Manager's Guide to Performance Management

Second Edition

Robert Bacal

McGraw-Hill

New York Chicago San Francisco Lisbon
London Madrid Mexico City Milan New Delhi
San Juan Seoul Singapore Sydney Toronto

1 2 3 4 5 6 7 8 9 0 DOC/DOC 1 6 5 4 3 2 1

ISBN   978-0-07-177225-9
MHID   0-07-177225-1

e-ISBN   978-0-07-177254-9
e-MHID   0-07-177254-5

Library of Congress Cataloging-in-Publication Data
Bacal, Robert.
  Performance management / by Robert Bacal. — 2nd ed.
    p. cm.
  Includes index.
  ISBN-13: 978-0-07-177225-9 (alk. paper)
  ISBN-10: 0-07-177225-1 (alk. paper)
  1. Employees—Rating of. 2. Performance standards. I. Title.
  HF5549.5.R3B285 2012
  658.3'125--dc23

                        2011041021

This is a CWL Publishing Enterprises book developed for McGraw-Hill by CWL Publishing Enterprises, Inc., Madison, Wisconsin, www.cwlpub.com.

Contents

Introduction

Right now a manager and an employee are meeting to discuss the employee's performance—a performance appraisal meeting, if you will. The manager would rather be doing something else. The employee would rather have multiple root canal surgeries without anesthetic. What's more, for every manager who's sitting down with an employee to evaluate performance, there's a manager who's trying to figure out how to avoid doing it—to avoid filling out the forms, having the meeting, communicating about performance—going through what seems like a paper chase of no value.

Most people dislike performance appraisals. Should we care? Should you care? Probably. Communication between manager and employee about performance is essential to increase productivity, improve staff morale and engagement, and allow coordination of each employee's work so it contributes to the goals of the company.

But many managers focus on the wrong things. They focus on *appraisal* rather than *planning*. They focus on a *one-way* flow of words (manager to employee) rather than *dialogue*. They focus on required *forms* rather than the *communication* needed for everyone to succeed. They focus on the *past* rather than the *present* and *future*. They focus on *blaming* rather than *solving problems*. As a result, what should be a cooperative effort between manager and employee turns into an awkward, stressful process both parties try to avoid.

It doesn't have to be that way. While many companies and managers don't get much value from the time they spend on performance management and appraisal, there are people who are reaping benefits from the process. How are they doing it? How do they make it work?

That's what this book is about. It's about reorienting ourselves—focusing on what organizations, managers, and employees need to succeed. It's about looking at performance appraisal and performance management as ways to engineer success for everyone. It's about understanding that performance management is a people process. It's about helping you learn to communicate cooperatively with staff to improve performance.

This book is not about theory. It's about doing all the things that make performance management work. It's time we looked at how performance management and appraisal can add value for the company, the manager, and the employee.

Why Read This Book?

Chances are you aren't getting full value from whatever you're doing to manage performance. That's why I wrote this book.

First, we help you see why you need to manage performance, focusing on *value*. What do you gain as a manager? How do employees benefit? How does your company gain? Second, by the end of the book you'll have figured out how to do it so it works. You'll learn the steps in the performance communication/management process. You'll learn how to turn it into a true dialogue. You'll learn how to turn even badly designed forms and procedures into something useful. And perhaps most important, you'll learn how to reduce the discomfort most people associate with performance management and performance appraisal.

Overview

The first three chapters in this book will help you understand where performance management fits into the broader scheme of things and the benefits of doing it well.

Chapter 1 presents an overview of the process, defines it, and explains the payoffs for managers, employees, and the organization. In Chapter 2 we tackle some of the challenges of performance management. You'll find out why so many people avoid it. You'll also find out what makes a performance management system work—and the consequences of systems that don't work. Chapter 3 discusses performance management as a system in which all the parts must work together. We relate performance management to other things in your company—to strategic planning, to discipline, and to training and employee development.

Once we've set the stage, we move on to doing it and doing it right.

Chapter 4 helps you prepare yourself and your employees for the performance management process. You need information to make it work. What information? We tell you. How do you prepare staff to work with you? We help you with that, too.

Chapter 5 deals with what may be the most important part of performance management—performance planning. You and each employee must determine what he or she is to accomplish, identify the bull's-eyes they should aim for. You'll learn to work together to create a common understanding.

Chapter 6 talks about ongoing performance communication. You cannot simply set performance targets and then wait until it's time for appraisals. That approach is deadly and guarantees failure. We present some options for formal and informal ways to communicate about employee performance during the year.

In Chapter 7 you'll find a process for gathering data, observing, and documenting. Performance management and appraisal should be based on more than opinion. It should be based on facts and observations. We talk about the need to document and communicate about performance so both you and the company have protection from malicious or unfair legal action.

In Chapters 8 and 9 we consider the performance appraisal and review process. You'll find a discussion of the merits and pitfalls associated with rating systems, ranking systems, and objective-based systems. We help you understand how you can conduct the performance review meeting so it's cooperative, and so you and the employee are on the same side—with both of you working to create value and success.

Chapter 10 talks about performance diagnosis and improvement.

How do you identify the causes of performance difficulties? Where do you look? How do you remove barriers to performance?

Sometimes managers need to take action when employees are consistently not meeting expectations. While performance management isn't used primarily for disciplinary reasons, it does play an important role in dealing with serious workplace problems and difficulties. In Chapter 11 you'll learn about progressive discipline, an often misunderstood process, and look at what you can do to address thorny employee situations.

Chapter 12 looks at questions managers have about performance management and provides answers, including some less traditional performance management methods.

Chapter 13 returns us to the central theme—that performance management is about creating value through relationships and effective communication. It isn't about forms or judging or categorizing employees. It's about people. In this chapter we talk about specific skills and things you can do to make it work.

In Chapter 14, we look at the role of the human resources department in assisting the organization to make performance management work. We look at ways it does work and how it can get in the way of creating an effective system.

In Chapter 15, we'll tackle the tough task of revamping or revitalizing an enterprisewide performance management system. It's a tough slog—a process of managing and implementing change, but it's essential if you want to move from sleepwalking through appraisals to providing tools that increase productivity for managers and employees, alike.

Finally, in Chapter 16, we pull it all together with a case study. You'll read about Acme Progressive and how the company used a performance management system to add value to its operations by creating a situation where each stakeholder receives value and perceives that value.

I don't believe it's possible to use a cookbook approach to performance management. There isn't one recipe that works for everyone. It's possible, though, to provide the principles and actions associated with successful performance management so you can make it work for your staff and your company. By the end of this book, you'll have a good grasp of the whys, hows, whens, and whats of performance management so you can develop a way to do it that helps everyone—you, your staff, and your organization.

Special Features

The idea behind the books in the Briefcase Series is to give you practical information written in a friendly person-to-person style. The chapters deal with tactical issues and include lots of examples. They also feature numerous sidebars designed to give you different types of specific information. Here's a description of the sidebars you'll find in this book.

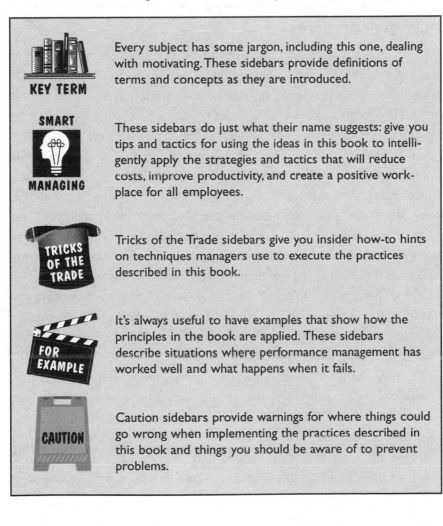

KEY TERM

Every subject has some jargon, including this one, dealing with motivating. These sidebars provide definitions of terms and concepts as they are introduced.

SMART MANAGING

These sidebars do just what their name suggests: give you tips and tactics for using the ideas in this book to intelligently apply the strategies and tactics that will reduce costs, improve productivity, and create a positive workplace for all employees.

TRICKS OF THE TRADE

Tricks of the Trade sidebars give you insider how-to hints on techniques managers use to execute the practices described in this book.

FOR EXAMPLE

It's always useful to have examples that show how the principles in the book are applied. These sidebars describe situations where performance management has worked well and what happens when it fails.

CAUTION

Caution sidebars provide warnings for where things could go wrong when implementing the practices described in this book and things you should be aware of to prevent problems.

How can you ensure you won't make a mistake when you're trying to implement the techniques the book describes? You can't completely, but these sidebars give you practical advice on how to minimize the possibility of things going wrong.

This icon identifies sidebars where you'll find specific procedures and techniques you can use to successfully implement the book's principles and practices.

TOOLS

Acknowledgments

I'm proud to say the first edition of this book has been continuously in print since 1998, so it's time to thank the people who have allowed me to have a "voice" on this subject, those who inspired or helped.

I'd like to thank the readers of all my books. You keep books in print. Without you, there would be no new books on any subject.

I'd also like to thank some of the famous and popular writers and consultants on this subject who continue to tell us we should scrap performance appraisals or use techniques (employee ranking, firing the bottom 10 percent) that have failed for decades. Such antiquated thinking! I'm not being facetious. The abundance of bad advice with roots buried deep in the past motivates me. We need performance management and appraisal approaches for *this* millennium, and dinosaurs can energize us to run in the opposite direction. That's a good thing. Let's run in the opposite direction together to create workplaces that are more productive, engaging, and successful. Performance management built on cooperation and working together is key.

A huge thanks to the thousands of managers, human resource professionals, and employees who have been open and honest enough with me to tell me what works and what doesn't work in the realm of performance management. I've learned almost everything I know from you, from both the well skilled and less skilled. An extra special thank you to the managers and executives I've worked for, who taught me through direct experience how a really effective performance management system can work (or not).

In appreciation of understanding my schedule and managing to live with delays in getting this book done, thank you to John Woods of CWL Publishing and the good folks at McGraw-Hill. By the way, John instigated the first edition of this book, my first book for a major publisher, back in 1998.

How can one thank one's long-suffering wife? Words cannot capture the contributions, support, and help she has provided.

Finally, a doff of the cap to two people who inspire me as human beings. OK. Sometimes strange human beings, but inspirational nonetheless. To Brian Barsky, professor at the University of California, Berkeley, whose curiosity, intensity, and unrelenting thinking are worthy of emulation. His commitment to accomplishing something in the real world has been awe inspiring. It's getting close to 50 years of friendship. That last quest was a humdinger, and you won. Wow.

And to Martin Webber and family who, among all my friends, model a sane, calm, grounded way of looking at the world that incorporates tolerance of risk and love of people around the world. To Ginger, David, Nate, and Martin, thanks. By the way, to both Brian and Martin: it's time to come back to Canada, eh!

Performance Management: An Overview

I t's year-end at Acme Progressive. Managers and employees are going through their yearly dance of performance appraisal, at least that's what they call it.

Michael manages 14 employees directly. No question he has a lot on his plate, meeting with staff, filling out forms, and gulping antacid. Since the personnel department pushes him to get his forms in on time, he has to figure out a way to get this all done as fast as possible.

And he does. He sends an appraisal form to each employee via interoffice mail. After employees complete the forms, he meets with each one for about 15 minutes to discuss the forms, and then signs them. Voilà! Problem solved. The paperwork gets done on time, the personnel department is content, and everyone goes back to their "real work." Except there's a problem.

What's Wrong with This Picture?

The better question might be, Is there anything right with this picture? Here's more information about Acme.

The forms Michael and the other managers send on to the personnel department are put into file folders and mostly forgotten. The information on the forms is so vague and unreliable it can't be used to make basic personnel decisions, let alone decisions about salary and promotions.

Michael and his staff won't look at them again until the next year-end performance appraisal dance. If you could hear Michael's staff talking privately about the process, you would hear comments like "What a joke!" or "This is a waste of time."

There's more. Michael's department doesn't run well. Staff miss deadlines. They aren't sure who should be doing what, and things fall through the cracks, while in other areas they step all over each other getting things done. Mistakes get repeated, which drives everybody nuts, but nobody seems to know why they keep happening. Not even Michael knows what's going on. All he knows is that he is so busy he can't keep up.

Here's the fundamental problem. Michael, his manager, colleagues, and employees consider "performance management" a necessary evil. They do it because they "ought to" or "have to." They don't realize that performance management, if carried out properly, has the potential to fix many of the problems they're facing.

While managing performance can have incredible power to solve many organizational problems, most managers learn to manage performance by having the process "done to them." They repeat the process, apply the same wrong mindset, and repeat the mistakes their own managers have made. They learned well. They learned the wrong things. It's all a waste. Not a smidgen of value here. No, it's worse than a waste. Employees think Michael is a poor manager (perhaps they're right) because they see *him* forcing them into a valueless process. That damages his credibility. The organization thinks it's accomplishing something, but it's only creating more useless work for people who have better things to do. They're doing it all wrong. Pure and simple.

Is There Hope?

Yes, there's hope. Acme has a skilled and dedicated staff. The managers are good folks and bright—even if they need to learn about managing performance. If they break away from existing habits, they can be much better at solving Acme's business problems and creating a work climate that's more engaging.

There's hope for every company and every manager. Does the Acme story sound familiar to you? Have you ever done what Michael did? Have you ever had your performance appraised in a way that didn't help you and discouraged you from wanting to improve at all? Probably. Are you getting value from your performance management system? A little? A lot? Probably less than you could get.

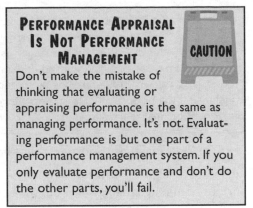

PERFORMANCE APPRAISAL IS NOT PERFORMANCE MANAGEMENT

CAUTION

Don't make the mistake of thinking that evaluating or appraising performance is the same as managing performance. It's not. Evaluating performance is but one part of a performance management system. If you only evaluate performance and don't do the other parts, you'll fail.

Our goal for this book is to explore the basic question, How can you use performance management as a meaningful tool to help people (and therefore your organization) succeed? If you help employees excel, you've added tremendous value to the proposition, and that changes the whole equation.

Let's start by looking at what performance management is and what it isn't.

Performance Management: What Is It?

Performance management is an ongoing communication process, undertaken in partnership between an employee and his or her immediate supervisor, that involves establishing clear, shared expectations and understanding about:

- the essential job functions the employee is expected to do
- how the employee's job contributes to the goals of the organization
- what "doing the job well" means in concrete terms
- how employee and supervisor will work together to sustain, improve, or build on existing employee performance
- how job performance will be measured
- identifying barriers to performance and removing them

That gives us a starting point, and we'll continue to flesh out things as we go. Note some important words here. *Performance management* is done *with* the employee because it benefits the employee, the manager, and the organization, and is best done in a collaborative, cooperative way. Performance management is a means of preventing poor performance

Performance management The ongoing communication process, undertaken in partnership between an employee and his or her immediate supervisor, that involves establishing **KEY TERM** clear expectations and understanding about the jobs to be done. It's a system with a number of components, all of which need to be included if the performance management system is to add value to the organization, managers, and staff.

and working together to improve performance. Above all, performance management means ongoing, two-way communication between the performance manager (supervisor or manager) and employee. It's about talking and listening. It's about both people learning and improving.

What Performance Management Isn't

It's important to know what performance management is, but we also need to know what it is not. In our tale about Acme Progressive, Michael thought that performance *appraisal* was the same as performance *management*. Most people at Acme thought performance management was about filling out and filing forms. No surprise that the process had no positive value.

To succeed at performance management, you need to be aware of some common misconceptions that can trip up even the best of managers.

Performance management isn't:

- something a manager does to an employee
- a club to force people to work better or harder
- used only in poor performance situations
- about completing forms once a year

It's an ongoing communication process between two people. That's the key point. Remember that it's about people working with people to make everyone better, and you *will* succeed.

What's the Payoff for Using Performance Management?

As you read more about performance management, you'll realize that it takes time and effort—perhaps time and effort you would rather use for other things. What manager wants more work? Consider, though, that the time and effort are an investment.

When performance management is used properly, there are clear benefits to everyone—managers, employees, and the organization. Let's take a look at these potential benefits.

For Managers

When I speak to managers about employee performance, I ask, "What things about your job drive you nuts, the things that you take home at the end of the day?" Here are some of their answers:

- feeling the need to micromanage and be involved in everything to make sure it goes right
- never having enough time in the day
- employees who are too timid to make decisions they could make on their own
- employees' lack of understanding of their jobs, particularly the whys of the jobs
- disagreements about who does what and who is responsible for what
- employees giving too little information to managers when information is important
- finding out about problems too late to prevent them from growing
- poor-quality performance
- employees repeating their mistakes

What common threads can we find in these complaints?

Let's start with micromanaging. One reason managers feel the need to be involved in everything is they aren't confident their employees are going to do the job the way the manager wants. Wouldn't it make more sense to make sure employees understand what's needed, rather than trying to be involved in everything?

How about not having enough time? When employees don't have a clear idea of what their jobs are, how they should be done, and why, that creates more work for managers. Decisions that employees could make end up on the manager's desk. Little problems that should never involve the manager keep coming up if employees don't understand their jobs well enough to feel they can make good decisions.

What's the common thread? Lack of clarity, lack of shared understanding, and not being on the same wavelength create more work.

What about staff not giving important information to the manager when it's needed? Managers need to know about problems before they get bigger in order to avoid difficulties rather than fighting fires. Besides, not having information can be embarrassing when your boss asks you how something is going.

SMART

MANAGING

WHAT KIND OF EMPLOYEES DO YOU VALUE?

Ask yourself: what kinds of employees do you want working for you? Describe their positive behaviors. If you track back, you'll find that performance management is the *essential* tool for creating the kinds of employees you want. Performance management creates the context in which employees can excel and, as a positive side effect, makes the manager's job easier.

Finally, let's turn to poor-quality performance and repetition of mistakes. If we have no way to help employees learn to be better performers, they *will* repeat mistakes and achieve less than they might. If we have no way to diagnose why mistakes happen, how can we hope to prevent them? We can't—and it's a pretty sure thing that the mistakes aren't going to go away on their own.

While performance management can't solve every problem, it has the potential to address many common management concerns. If you use it properly, invest the time, and create cooperative relationships, performance management can:

- Reduce your need to be involved in every activity (micromanagement).
- Save time by helping employees make decisions on their own by ensuring they have the necessary knowledge and understanding to make decisions properly (employee empowerment).
- Reduce time-consuming misunderstandings among staff about who is responsible for what.
- Reduce the frequency of situations where you don't have the information you need when you need it.
- Reduce mistakes and errors (and their repetition) by helping you and your staff identify the causes of errors or inefficiencies.

- Provide context and meaning for employees, thus increasing employee engagement and motivation.

To summarize, performance management is an investment up front so that you can get out of the way and let your employees do their jobs. They'll know what they're expected to do, what decisions they can make on their own, how well they have to do their jobs, and when you need to be involved. This will allow you to attend to tasks that only you can address. That saves time.

For Employees

If performance management is a process done in partnership with staff, we need to address how it benefits staff members. After all, it's hardly realistic to expect employees to participate in a partnership if there are no payoffs for them.

Just as we did for managers, let's look at some common things that drive employees nuts:

- not knowing whether they are doing well or not
- not knowing what level of authority they have
- not getting recognition for a job well done
- not having an opportunity to develop new skills
- finding out the boss has been dissatisfied with an employee's work for a long time
- being unable to make even simple decisions by themselves
- being micromanaged
- not having the resources they need to do their jobs

Performance management can address these concerns. It can provide scheduled opportunities to discuss work progress, so employees receive the feedback they need to assess their accomplishments and know where they stand. That regular communication ensures there are no surprises at the end of the year. Since performance management helps employees understand what they should be doing and why, it gives them a degree of empowerment—the ability to make day-to-day decisions. Finally, a critical part of the performance management process is figuring out how to improve performance, even if there is no current performance problem. This provides an opportunity for employees to develop new skills while

TRICKS OF THE TRADE

Explaining the Point to Your Staff

Like managers, employees need to understand the value of performance management and how it will help *them*. If they don't understand that, they're unlikely to enter into partnership to make it work. Explain the process and how it will benefit the employees. Ask them how it can be made better so it helps them even more. Not only must performance management have value, but employees need to *perceive* it has value.

identifying unexamined barriers to increased productivity.

In sum, employees benefit from better understanding their jobs and responsibilities. Knowing their parameters, they can act more freely.

For the Organization

Organizations work more effectively when the goals and objectives of the organization, those of the smaller work units, and the job responsibilities of each employee are all linked. When people in the organization understand how their work contributes to the success of the company, morale and productivity usually improve. A company can have all its parts aimed at the same bull's-eye. Performance management is the key to making these connections clear to everyone.

There's another reason why performance management is important. It's a legal reason—and a serious one.

Municipalities, states or provinces, and federal governments have established laws, regulations, and guidelines that organizations must follow when hiring and terminating employees. The intent is to address various forms of workplace discrimination. Though laws differ according to jurisdiction, you can count on one thing: these rules apply to you.

If you have to fire an employee for poor performance, he or she may have legal recourse to challenge that action. The employee could claim the firing was based on some form of discrimination (gender, age, ethnic background) and/or that no warning was given so there was no chance to improve. If a labor grievance or civil suit is filed, the organization must defend its actions with evidence of poor performance. The evidence must be as objective and specific as possible. In a later chapter we map out exactly what that means.

A properly constructed performance management system includes documenting performance problems in a timely way, tracking how those

---

PROTECTION FROM FALSE ALLEGATIONS

John was an account executive with a public relations firm. While initially John was moderately successful, his sales declined during the past year. After the first quarter of lower sales, his boss, Dave, met with John, went over the figures, and worked with him to identify possible causes and develop some ideas for improvement. Dave kept records of the meeting and the sales figures.

Unfortunately, despite the meeting and subsequent attempts to resolve the issue, John's sales continued to drop. After trying everything to remedy the situation, Dave decided to let John go. Although John couldn't deny the drop in sales, he felt that his termination was not due to poor performance, but because he belonged to a minority. He threatened to file a complaint with the appropriate government agency.

The parties and their attorneys met, and the company provided the detailed documentation of performance problems and Dave's efforts to work with John to solve them. After the meeting, John's attorney advised him that no court would rule in his favor and the complaint was dropped. The evidence compiled through proper performance management prevented a costly legal battle that could have damaged the company's reputation in the eyes of its customers.

---

problems are communicated to the employee, and recording all positive steps taken to remedy the situation. Not only are records critical in a formal hearing, but the existence of proper records discourages employees from taking frivolous or nuisance-type actions.

Manager's Checklist for Chapter 1

☑ Performance management is an ongoing communication between the manager and each employee to clarify job responsibilities and improve performance continuously.

☑ All parties in a partnership need to know why they are partnering. If you understand the advantages of performance management, you can explain to staff how it will benefit them so they can buy into it.

☑ Don't confuse performance management with performance appraisal. Appraisal is only one part of a performance management system. Managing performance requires that you use all of the components to succeed.

☑ The key to changing your performance management system is to create value for all stakeholders and work to alter the perceptions of stakeholders so that performance management is seen as more positive.

The Challenge of Performance Management

I f performance management were easy, every company would reap the benefits. Every manager would look forward with happy anticipation to performance planning and appraisal meetings, and every employee would jump at the chance to review his or her performance with the manager. Human resources departments wouldn't nag managers to do reviews.

Rare? Yes. Possible for you? Yes!

The challenge you face is to find a way to do performance management that makes sense to you and your employees, gets you what you need to do your job, helps employees do their jobs, and helps the company achieve its goals. Whether you receive a set of forms and procedures from your company or you're creating your own way to manage performance, you still need to understand what separates a good approach from a poor one. Some basic psychology helps, too, because performance management is about relationships, communication, and people. If you understand why managers and employees dread traditional performance management, you can come up with solutions to minimize the discomfort and clear the way for a system that's perceived as adding value for everyone. These are the things we discuss in this chapter.

EVEN THE BEST ARE CHALLENGED

FOR EXAMPLE   I got a call from a famous high-tech firm, a company whose products you probably use every day and whose name you would immediately recognize. The company has been highlighted as a leader, an example of great management. But management was struggling with a problem.

Only about half of the managers were turning in their performance management documents. The company wanted to know how to get better buy-in and compliance.

My advice? Forget about compliance. Instead, build commitment, so employees want to complete the documents because they're useful. Educate managers and employees about how performance management can help them reach their job and career goals.

Why Do So Many People Try to Avoid Performance Management?

Many managers end up so skilled at *not* managing performance that they never get the process done, despite prodding from those human resources folks. Relieved employees don't push the point.

Managers' Reluctance

You're the best judge of why you are uncomfortable using performance management and performance appraisal. But here are a few reasons often cited by managers.

- The forms and procedures my company makes me use don't make much sense—it's just a whole lot of pointless paperwork.
- I don't have the time.
- I hate getting into arguments with employees. No matter what I do, employees feel attacked. It's never pleasant.
- I have trouble giving feedback to staff or even knowing what they're doing. I can't be watching them all the time.

Forms, computer programs, and procedures that don't make sense. Many companies insist that managers use a set of forms, specific software, a specific method, and/or a schedule that doesn't fit every situation. Human resources is often the custodian of these methods and prescribes how it is to be done. Are managers consulted? No. Are employees asked what would be useful? No. Surprise, surprise! Having a system imposed doesn't usually create ownership, investment, and understanding of the value of the system, even if it's a good one.

If you're stuck with forms or an approach you don't like, don't give up. No performance management system is perfect, ever! When you focus on performance management as a way to communicate and build relationships, the format of the reporting system becomes less important. Work to clarify job expectations with each employee, create a climate of trust and working together, involve employees as partners, and aim your discussions at creating success for everyone and you can make it work.

(And if you're in a position of having input into companywide programs, you might want to involve managers in designing the system.)

No time! Yes, performance management takes time. But when managers plead "no time to do it," it's because they misunderstand what performance management can offer. A common misconception about performance management is that it's about after-the-fact discussions—catching mistakes and poor performance after they happen. But that's not the core of performance management. It's not about inspection or looking in the rearview mirror to assign blame. It's about preventing problems and identifying barriers to success before they become costly.

> **SMART MANAGING**
>
> **DON'T LIKE THE COMPANY APPROACH?**
> Companies tend to want a uniform process to manage performance, which can make the process overly bureaucratic. If you don't find the mandated approach useful, develop a way to make it work by focusing on the opportunity to discuss performance with employees, person to person. If you focus on building relationships, involving employees as equals, and communicating, you can make even a bad system work better.

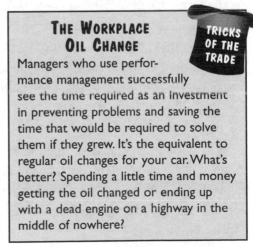

> **TRICKS OF THE TRADE**
>
> **THE WORKPLACE OIL CHANGE**
> Managers who use performance management successfully see the time required as an investment in preventing problems and saving the time that would be required to solve them if they grew. It's the equivalent to regular oil changes for your car. What's better? Spending a little time and money getting the oil changed or ending up with a dead engine on a highway in the middle of nowhere?

Performance management can save management time. When employees don't have clear expectations about what they are to do, when, and how well, they involve managers in issues they could handle themselves. Or they make mistakes because they think they know what to do but don't really know. When employees make inappropriate decisions, they create brush fires (or forest fires) that require management intervention.

As the commercial goes, you can pay now or pay a lot more later.

Fear of confrontation. Managers express concern about bringing up performance problems because they fear confrontation, and appraisal feels like confrontation.

Sometimes that happens, but it isn't the norm, and it shouldn't be the norm. Here's why:

- When employees see performance management as a process designed to help rather than to blame, they're much more likely to be cooperative and open.

- Discussions about performance shouldn't be limited to the manager passing judgment on the employee. Employees should be encouraged to evaluate themselves. Manager and employee get to exchange views on performance. Often, employees are actually more critical of their own work than the manager is.

- If managers look at performance management as something they do to employees, confrontation is inevitable. If managers view it as a partnership, they reduce confrontation.

- Performance management is not about discussing poor performance. It's talking about accomplishments, successes, and improvement. Focus on these three things and you will reduce confrontation because manager and employee are on the same side.

- When confrontation occurs or becomes ugly, it's often because managers have avoided dealing with a problem until it's severe. Early identification of problems helps in the resolution process.

While it's understandable that managers worry about confrontation, that fear is often a result of looking at performance management as a "me versus them" dichotomy. Set an appropriate climate, use effective interpersonal skills, and stop procrastinating, and you will reduce conflict and confrontation.

Feedback and observation problems. Some managers complain they can't give feedback to staff because they don't have time to stand over them and watch them do their jobs every day. It's a good point. You can't stand there watching, because you don't have the time—and because you will drive your employees around the bend. So let each employee be the expert on his or her job and performance.

In some rare situations it may be necessary to observe employees as they work. For the most part, your role isn't to judge them, but to help them assess their own work as they go. You and each staff member will work together to find the answers.

> **REDUCING CONFLICT POTENTIAL**   **SMART**
>
>
>
> **MANAGING**
>
> Smart managers know how to reduce conflict. Approach the process as a "we" exercise. Don't give pronouncements on performance, but first engage the employee in self-evaluation. Also, help employees understand how performance management can help them reach their goals. Offer to help, and find out what the employee needs to improve.

Employees' Reluctance

Managers are employees, too. You already know some of the reasons why employees feel uncomfortable with performance management because you've been there, too.

As a manager, you're responsible for helping employees feel more at ease with the process. What might make an employee feel uncomfortable? Consider the following:

> **DON'T DELAY**   **SMART**
>
> **MANAGING**
>
> Think of performance management as a problem-prevention technique. Focus on the time you save by preventing problems. If you set a climate of working with staff to do things right, performance and relationships will improve. Then you don't have to procrastinate any more. And remember: the goal is to help staff learn to assess their own work, which will save you time.

- Many employees have had poor experiences with performance management, perhaps with other managers.
- Nobody likes to be criticized. Employees may have experienced situations where their manager gave them no feedback until their yearly review and then dumped on them.

■ When employees don't know what to expect, they become fearful. That can also make them aggressive or put them on the defensive.

■ Employees don't understand the point of performance management or don't see it as something useful to them.

These are things you can do something about. Later in the book we talk about specific techniques to help staff develop positive perceptions of the performance management process. For now, remember that your job includes educating staff so they understand how they can benefit. Remember also that initial discomfort is normal and can be overcome.

Criteria for Performance Management That Works

As a manager, you will make choices about performance management (and there are many) that will determine how well it works and whether it returns value. Knowing what makes a performance management system work will guide you in making those decisions. We help you address some of the important questions, but here are a few examples.

■ How do I communicate my expectations about employee job responsibilities?

■ How do I involve staff as partners?

■ How do I broach the subject of poor performance?

■ How often do I need to meet with staff?

■ How do I make performance management meaningful for everyone?

Our starting point is to state what we mean by an *effective performance management system*. An effective system helps organizations, managers, and employees succeed. It helps the organization meet its short- and long-term goals and objectives by helping managers and employees do their jobs better. Since performance management is a tool for success, we must look

TRICKS OF THE TRADE

A WONDERFUL QUESTION Need a way to open a discussion about performance management with employees? Explain that you need to discuss their jobs to help them improve. Ask them, "Since we need to meet on a regular basis, what do you need from me at those meetings to help you do your job better?" Meet those needs and you quickly put everybody on the same performance management team.

at what organizations, managers, and employees need to succeed. Only then can we understand what an effective performance management system will look like. Let's look at each need separately.

> **Effective performance management system** A process that helps the organization meet its **KEY TERM** short- and long-term goals and objectives by helping managers and employees do their jobs better and better.

What Organizations Need to Succeed

There are five factors in organizational success:

1. Organizations need to coordinate the work of their units (divisions, departments, branches) so all are aimed at achieving the same goals and purposes.
2. Organizations need ways to identify barriers as they arise, catch problems early, and prevent problems. Whether those barriers are individual (staff members who lack needed skills) or related to systems (poorly designed work flow or too much bureaucracy), they need to be identified and addressed as soon as possible.
3. Organizations also need to conform to legal requirements regarding employment so they're protected.
4. Organizations need a way to gather information to make important human resources decisions. Who should be promoted? Are there special areas where training is needed?
5. Organizations need to be continuously developing their people (both managers and employees) so they can make the organization more competitive.

What Managers Need to Succeed

As a manager, no doubt you have a pretty good idea about what helps you do your job well and what you need. But here are a few things to consider.

- Managers need information about what's going on in their organization—what's going well, what's going less well, the status of schedules and projects, and so on. You want to get the right amount of information (not too much, not too little) when you need it (not too early, not too late).

■ To help staff improve, managers need information about how well each employee is performing his or her job and how each can improve. If the performance is poor, managers need to know why problems are occurring.

■ Just as with organizations, managers need to direct all employees, to harness the energy and skills of each employee and coordinate their efforts to achieve goals.

■ Managers need a way to help employees feel motivated and valued. That means having ways to recognize good performance and to help everyone succeed.

■ Managers need a way to communicate job expectations to employees—what's important and less important, and the kinds of decisions employees can make on their own. Why? Because employees need to know those things to succeed.

■ Managers need to document performance problems for two reasons. First, if managers can't be specific about performance problems, they're not likely to be able to help an employee improve. Second, managers may be expected to justify disciplinary action with precise, specific data about performance difficulties or violation of workplace rules.

What Employees Need to Succeed

Now let's look at what employees need to perform their jobs successfully.

■ Employees need to know what you expect them to do, when, and how well. If they don't know, how can they succeed?

■ Employees need regular, specific feedback on their job performance. They need to know where they are excelling and where they could improve. If they don't know what they should continue to do and what they should change, how can they get better?

■ Employees need to understand how their work fits in with the work of others, the goals of their work unit, and the overall mission and purpose of the company. Why? Because it's motivating to feel part of a larger purpose and to have a sense of helping to achieve that purpose. Meaning creates employee engagement.

■ Employees need to play an active role in defining and redefining their jobs. First, it's motivating to do so. Second, employees, particularly experienced ones, know their jobs better than anyone else and know best how to remove barriers to their success.

- Employees need to know their levels of authority. When they know what decisions they can make on their own, what decisions need to involve others, and what decisions are managerial, they can operate with greater confidence. This knowledge also speeds up processes.

- Employees need to have opportunities to develop their skills and grow. An employee learning new things and applying them is more likely to stick around and more likely to be motivated.

Our Performance Management Criteria

Now we can link our criteria for an effective performance management approach to what organizations, managers, and employees need to suc ceed. Performance management should provide:

1. A means of coordinating work so that the goals and objectives of the organization, units, and employees are aimed at the same bull's-eye.
2. A way to identify problems in processes that keep the organization from becoming more effective.
3. A way to document performance problems so the company con- forms to laws and guidelines (and demonstrates that conformance), to discourage frivolous lawsuits and grievances, and to serve as evi- dence, if necessary.
4. Information for making decisions about promotions, employee development strategies, and training.
5. Information so managers and supervisors can prevent problems, help staff do their jobs, coordinate work, and report to their bosses in a complete, knowledgeable way (so they don't look stupid!).
6. A way for managers to work with employees to identify problem areas, diagnose the causes, and take action to eliminate the problems
7. A means of coordinating the work of all the employees who report to the same manager.
8. A method of providing regular, ongoing feedback to employees in a way that supports their motivation.
9. A means of preventing mistakes by clarifying expectations, establish- ing shared understanding of what employees can and can't do on their own, and showing how each employee's job fits into the big picture.

10. A means of planning employee development and training activities.

SMART MANAGING

ADDRESSING THE WHOLE CHALLENGE

Think of the performance management process as a system. If you do, you can handle it in a way that meets essential needs while keeping it practical. Focus on the overall purpose. Sometimes trade-offs are necessary. By understanding what performance management is for and how it works, you can make intelligent decisions about the process.

These 10 points aim the performance management system at the goal of improving the organization and everyone's performance. There are a few more points to cover.

We need the performance management system to be practical. If the process is so unwieldy that nobody wants to use it, it's not worth much. Let's add a few more practical criteria for the system:

- It should be as simple as possible.
- It should require the least amount of paperwork and bureaucracy possible.
- It should require the least time investment possible.
- It needs to maximize comfort—or at least minimize discomfort.
- It must serve the needs of managers, employees, and the organization. If managers or employees see it as a waste of time, it isn't going to be effective.

When Performance Management Approaches Don't Work

Let's end this chapter by talking about what happens when performance management approaches are badly designed, aren't used properly, or are ineffective.

People feel that lousy performance management systems are harmless. That's not true. A poorly implemented approach can be much worse than having none at all. In fact, if you can't or won't do performance management properly, don't even try. If it isn't helping to increase success, then it's probably causing damage.

What kinds of damage? First, a poor performance management system undermines the credibility of management. When employees con-

---

A POOR SYSTEM IN ACTION

Jean struggled with one of her employees, who was often late, missed work, made a lot of mistakes, and treated customers badly. After meeting with the employee several times, Jean finally fired him.

FOR EXAMPLE

The employee appealed the firing, claiming that it was unfair and not based on any performance failure, because Jean had been using a simple annual report card that rated performance from poor to excellent.

When the case went to court, the company was asked to produce data to justify termination for poor performance, including dates, details, and how each problem had been communicated to the employee. Jean had only a record of absences and a few annual ratings. The company lost the case because the court deemed there was insufficient evidence to prove poor performance.

---

sider the system a waste of time or a joke (which they often do), they also wonder about the intelligence of the managers who use that system. This situation hurts morale. Unfair systems alienate employees, as do systems that pit manager against employee. Good systems solve problems; poor systems create them.

Poor systems waste the time of employees, managers, and human resources departments. If you're going to spend time doing it, do it right.

Poor systems and execution provide a false sense of security. The legal system or a labor-management agreement requires certain kinds of documentation when disciplinary action is initiated. Poor systems may not provide the necessary information. Managers can find themselves caught in a situation in which they're helpless to deal with severe performance problems.

In the next chapter we discuss and evaluate various methods used to manage performance.

Manager's Checklist for Chapter 2

☑ To work, your performance management approach must be useful to the organization, to you, and—perhaps most important—to your employees. The only reason to use performance management is to help everybody be more successful.

☑ Some performance management systems work well. Many do not.

We can make them work by being clear about what constitutes a good system and what allows it to work.

☑ A poor performance management system is harmful. Decide whether you are willing to do it right (and invest in it) or you are going through the motions. If you aren't prepared to do it right, it's better not to do it at all.

☑ The challenge of performance management is finding ways to do it that are practical and meaningful. This requires thought and understanding.

Performance Management as a System

I f you want maximum results from performance management, view it as a system that operates within a larger system. I'll explain what this means in a moment.

First, let's look at why the concept of a "system" is important. We've talked about the consequences of poor performance management systems, the potential for damage, and the time and resources wasted when performance management is done badly. We've also pointed out that one of the major reasons why so many performance management efforts fail is they aren't connected to anything else in the workplace. They aren't connected to job success, performance improvement, employee development, the goals of the organization, or any other important parts of the organization. They just dangle. It's no wonder people don't see the point.

The other reason for failure? Managers don't use all the tools of performance management. If you believe that performance *appraisal* is performance *management*, it's just not going to work.

What Is a System?

A *system* has component parts that interact and work together in an interdependent way to accomplish something.

Take computer *systems*, for example. They consist of parts (monitor, video card, printer, memory, keyboard, and so on) that work together (at

System A set of components that work together
in an interdependent way
KEY TERM   to accomplish something.
Systems take inputs and, through a
series of processes, transform those
inputs into outputs—products, services,
or information.

least in theory!) to accomplish
tasks. The parts are interdependent. If you upgrade the central
processing unit (CPU), for
example, you won't realize the
full benefits unless you have
enough memory, because the
CPU and the memory interact.

Performance management is a system just like your computer system. Focus on only one part of the system and it won't work. We need to
discuss two questions:

1. What are the essential parts of an effective performance management system?
2. How can we integrate or link a performance management system to
   the rest of the organization's functions so it's relevant, meaningful,
   and contributes to the overall organization?

The Components of a Performance Management System

An important point: a performance management system isn't a linear
process.

Imagine a staircase. When you climb the stairs, you put your foot on the
first step, then on the next, and so on. Once you've reached the fifth step,
you don't usually jump back down to the first one. That's a straight-line
process: you start at step A, go to step B, and then to step C, and so forth.

Performance management isn't like that. In performance management

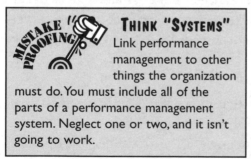

THINK "SYSTEMS"
Link performance
management to other
things the organization
must do. You must include all of the
parts of a performance management
system. Neglect one or two, and it isn't
going to work.

you might start at step A, move
to step B, and then back to step
A, sometimes having a foot on
two steps at the same time.
Why? Because it's not a
sequential process. It's a dynamic process between two
people that changes over time.

If this sounds confusing to you, it will be clearer as we describe all the components and how they fit together. In later chapters we explain how to successfully execute each of the parts of the performance management system. For now we'll keep these descriptions short.

Performance Planning

Performance planning is the usual point for an employee and manager to begin the performance management process. Manager and employee work together to identify what the employee should be doing for the period being planned, how well the work should be done, why it needs to be done, when it should be done, and other specifics, such as level of authority and decision making for the employee. Usually performance planning is done for a one-year period, but it can be revisited during that year.

By the end of the performance planning process, both manager and employee should be able to answer the following questions in the same way:

- What are the employee's major responsibilities for the year?
- How will we know whether the employee is succeeding?
- If appropriate, when should the employee carry out those responsibilities (e.g., for specific projects)?
- What level of authority does the employee have with respect to job tasks?
- Which job responsibilities are of most importance and which are of least importance?
- How do the employee's responsibilities contribute to the department or company?
- Why is the employee doing what he or she is doing?
- How will the manager help the employee accomplish the tasks?
- How will the manager and the employee work to overcome any barriers?
- Does the employee need to develop new skills/abilities to accomplish tasks (development planning)?
- How will the manager and the employee communicate during the year about job tasks, to prevent problems and keep current?

KEY TERM

Performance planning Starting point for performance management: employee and manager work together to identify, understand, and agree on what the employee is to do, how well it needs to be done, why, when, and so on.

While performance planning is mostly about clarifying job tasks for individual employees, it can provide a forum for discussing general issues. Some managers may want employees to understand that they are expected to refrain from insulting behavior toward their colleagues, to dress appropriately, and so on. Performance planning can reference these.

Process. People vary in how they go about creating a common understanding of the questions listed above. Almost always there will be at least one meeting between the manager and each employee. Sometimes group meetings can be used to make specific project assignments, followed by more detailed, individual meetings. Managers also use different resource materials: some will have employees look at the company's plan for the future before discussing individual roles, while others will start with the formal job description or a review of the work unit's goals.

Result. What comes out of performance planning besides "common understanding"? Usually the answers to the questions listed previously are written down in the form of objectives, goals, and standards. This constitutes the employee's plan for the year, which is then used in the performance appraisal meeting at the end of the period being planned. If employees need development or training to do their jobs, that's also recorded. The format of the plan can vary, but usually this document should be short, clear, and concise—no longer than several pages. Employee and manager both sign the form, signifying agreement with its contents.

Ongoing Performance Communication

Once each employee knows what to do, when, and how well, is that it until performance reviews at the end of the year? *No!*

Employees and organizations can't run on autopilot. Things change. Projects pop up unexpectedly. Perhaps employee and manager misjudged the time needed to complete a task. Maybe problems occur. We need to treat the *performance planning documents* as dynamic and we need to treat *job performance* as dynamic so we can remove barriers to performance before they occur or as they occur, *not* months later or at the end of the year.

Ongoing performance communication is a two-way process to track progress, identify barriers, and share information both parties need to succeed.

Process. The methods you use to foster that two-way communication will reflect what is needed to promote success in your workplace. Here are some common methods:

- short monthly or weekly status report meetings with each employee
- regular group meetings, in which every employee reports on the status of his or her projects and jobs
- regular short written status reports from each employee
- informal communication (e.g., manager walks around and chats with each employee)
- specific communication when problems crop up, at the discretion of the employee

You can see there's quite a range here in terms of the level of formality, from writing regular reports to just chatting. Is there a best way to do it? No. Clearly, if you had weekly individual meetings and you supervise 25 employees, that's all you'd be doing from sunrise to sunset. You have to decide when, how, and how often, based on what *both* you and the employee need to succeed. You might even find you need to communicate differently with different staff members. Some may need more involvement on your part and some less. Some jobs

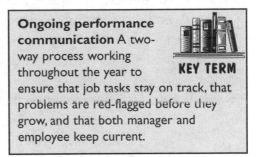

Ongoing performance communication A two-way process working throughout the year to **KEY TERM** ensure that job tasks stay on track, that problems are red-flagged before they grow, and that both manager and employee keep current.

require more communication than others. Use your common sense (and that of the employee) to determine the best way to do it so it's practical and meaningful. Don't set up communication methods that are impossible to carry out.

Result. In some cases, you may not need to produce anything on paper. After all, it's a communication process. In other situations, you may feel that some sort of paper trail is required. Some managers keep a few notes regarding job status and progress, or keep track of formal regular status meetings. Again, what you record or document depends on your needs. Rather than discuss that here, let's move on to the next component, which we call data gathering, observation, and documentation.

Data Gathering, Observation, and Documentation

Whether your concern is helping employees improve, disciplining an unproductive employee, or improving the way work is done, you need data or information to make decisions—and to justify your decisions if necessary. If you want to help an employee improve, you need to know where improvement is needed, where improvement is possible. For legal reasons, if you discipline an employee, you need some proof that he or she isn't performing at an appropriate level. And perhaps most important, if you want to improve the efficiency and productivity of your organization, how do you know where to look and what to change? You need information.

Data gathering is the process of getting information relevant to improvement, whether individual or organizational.

Observation is a way to gather data. For example, if you walk by the switchboard and hear phones ringing and unanswered, you've *observed* something. That's data. It doesn't tell you what the problem is or how to fix it, but it tells you something could be improved.

Documentation is the process of recording the data gathered so that it's available for use, so it isn't lost. If, when you observe the phones ringing, you write down the time, date, and circumstances, you've documented something.

Let's not make the mistake of thinking that we pay attention to and document only "bad things." We also need to pay attention to the good things, the successes and accomplishments. Imagine that you walk by a customer who is yelling at an employee, and you see that, in a very short time, the employee calms the customer down in a professional and constructive way. You may want to make a mental note of that, or even document it, so you can commend the employee and/or use that information to support a pay raise.

Process. Data gathering, observation, and documentation need to be done according to what's practical and realistic in your workplace. Here are some methods managers use:

- regularly observing by walking around (informal)
- collecting data and information from individual employees at status review meetings
- reviewing work produced by employees
- collecting actual data (e.g., the amount of time it takes to serve each customer, turnaround time, product development, or manufacturing time)
- asking for information (successes/problems) at staff meetings

We need to be careful about this process so we don't create unintentional and destructive side effects. Let's understand the mindset.

There are several reasons to gather data and document. The most important, and the one you should focus on, is organizational and individual

> **Data gathering, observation, and documentation**
> Data gathering is collecting information about the per-   **KEY TERM**
> formance of the organization or individuals for the purpose of improving performance. Observation is one means by which a manager can gather data. Documentation is recording the information collected.

improvement. To solve problems, you need to identify and understand them. That requires information. The other reason to gather data and document is to protect both the employee and the employer in the event of disagreement. If you need to prove to someone that the phone rang too many times or that a project wasn't completed, then you need data for support, perhaps times and dates.

Unfortunately, these two purposes can conflict. And which one you focus on will determine how you gather data and document. If you focus on protection against lawsuits and take the position your staff isn't trustworthy, you might feel you have to watch them all the time. That's not good. You don't have time for that. Do employees want the boss standing over them all day? No. It creates a bad work climate where productivity and morale suffer. If, however, you begin from the position of trusting staff, you don't have to stand over them and watch. That means staff can gather information and you don't have to rely solely on your own observations. This puts you and staff on the same side. You need to be clear about what you are trying to achieve.

Needless to say, we think the better choice is to trust staff and work with them. Frankly, watching over your staff just isn't practical and isn't a good use of your time. Instead, bring the staff into the data-gathering and improvement process.

Result. What you actually produce depends on what you need. Some people might use special forms to record their observations, while others might scribble them on napkins. You need to determine how much documentation to keep and what form it should take, depending on your answer to the following question: "What records do I need to keep to meet the goals I have set?" If you keep documentation, make sure you know *why* you are keeping it. Don't document just for the sake of doing it. That's a waste of time—unless you're preparing for a career as a private investigator.

AVOID NEGATIVE SIDE EFFECTS

CAUTION

Unintentional side effects (e.g., anger, lowered productivity, interpersonal problems) occur when we forget why we're managing performance and get caught up in following "the book" or "the formula." Always be clear about what you're trying to accomplish. Then, before acting, consider both the positive effects of an action and the possible negative side effects. For example, observing staff may provide good information, but it may also send the message that you don't trust their ability or competence.

Performance Appraisal Meetings

Now we've arrived at what most people think is the sum total of performance management, the performance appraisal process. Let's repeat the point once more: if *all* you do is appraisal, if you don't do planning and have ongoing communication, collect data, and diagnose problems, you're wasting your time.

The performance appraisal process involves manager and employee working together to assess the progress that the employee has made toward the goals set in performance planning, and to summarize what has gone well during the period under review and what has gone less well.

But it can be much more than that. It's a communication process, a forum for discussion that doesn't have to focus only on the individual employee. You can use the forum to uncover processes and procedures in the company that are inefficient, unproductive, or destructive. So the review meeting should *not* be only about evaluating the employee. It's an opportunity to solve problems.

The performance appraisal process provides:

- feedback to the employee that's formal, regular, and recorded
- documentation for a personnel file that may be used for determining promotions, pay levels, bonuses, disciplinary actions, etc.
- an opportunity to identify how performance can be improved, regardless of current level
- an opportunity to recognize strengths and successes
- a springboard for planning performance for the next year
- information about how employees might continue to develop
- an opportunity for a manager to identify additional ways to help employees in the future
- an opportunity to identify processes and procedures that are ineffective and costly

Process. There are a number of ways to do performance appraisal meetings. In a later chapter I'll walk you through the process and principles, but for now here's a brief overview.

First, prepare prior to the meeting. That might include the manager and employee doing independent appraisals on their own, reviewing objectives and standards, compiling questions, and so on. The preparation should shorten the time needed in the meeting and help both the manager and the employee refresh their memories.

During the meeting, the manager and employee work together to come to agreement on the employee's performance during the past year. They try to stick to specifics and use data rather than vague recollections. Where problems have occurred, the focus isn't on blaming, but on identifying the cause of the problem and formulating a strategy (see the Performance Diagnosis and Coaching section later in this chapter) to

KEY TERM **Performance appraisal meeting** A process where manager and employee work together to assess the degree to which the employee has attained agreed-on goals, and work together to overcome difficulties encountered. Also called "performance review meeting" or "performance evaluation meeting." Usually refers to an annual meeting.

prevent the problem from recurring.

Some managers combine a performance appraisal meeting with performance planning, so the performance management cycle is complete. So, in that situation, you review the past year's performance, and then set objectives and standards for the upcoming year. (Warning: this may result in long, tiring meetings.)

Results. The discussions in the performance appraisal meeting need to be documented. There are a number of ways to do that, depending on what the company demands and what is useful to manager and employee. For example, some companies require that some sort of rating form be used to summarize the performance appraisal discussions. Others may have more flexible forms or provide leeway regarding what the manager must send on to the personnel office. In any event, there *must* be documentation. Generally, that documentation is signed by both parties. In some cases, where manager and employee disagree with what is written down, the employee may add comments to indicate his or her disagreement.

Finally, if the manager is combining performance planning with performance appraisal, the plan (including goals, objectives, job tasks) will also be produced.

Performance Diagnosis and Coaching

Diagnosing performance issues and it's companion, coaching, occur throughout the entire performance management cycle—in other words all year long whenever there is room for improvement. Think "diagnosis" and "treatment" if that helps. They're the problem-solving component of performance management, the engine by which performance is improved in an ongoing way.

When some sort of problem is identified—whether it's an employee not achieving what was agreed upon or a department falling short—it's critical to determine *why* that problem occurred. Without diagnosing the root cause of the problem, how can we prevent it from happening again? We can't.

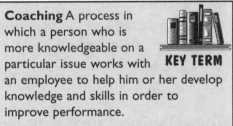

Performance diagnosis The process of problem solving and communication used to identify the under- **KEY TERM** lying causes of performance problems or deficits for an individual, a department, or even the whole organization.

For example, if employees don't achieve their objectives, there could be various causes for that performance deficit. Do they lack the skills needed? Didn't they work hard enough? Are they poorly organized? Or maybe the cause has little or nothing to do with the employees. Did other people in the organization withhold needed resources? Were the raw materials needed not available? Was the manager unclear about what needed to be done? So, problem diagnosis is vital—and it should be a continuous part of the performance management process.

Once the cause of a performance deficit is identified, manager and employee (and perhaps others in the organization) need to work together to remove the barriers and prevent the deficit. When a

Coaching A process in which a person who is more knowledgeable on a particular issue works with **KEY TERM** an employee to help him or her develop knowledge and skills in order to improve performance.

manager plays the role of mentor, teacher, or helper, we usually call that coaching. The manager works with the employee to help him or her develop knowledge and skills in order to improve performance.

Why is this important? Too often managers jump to unwarranted conclusions, blame the employee, and leave it to him or her to figure out how to fix the problem. Some managers take the position that it's solely the employee's responsibility to improve. It may be an interesting philosophical point, but it isn't practical.

Most employees want to improve. Sometimes they need help. Smart managers know that a small investment in occasional coaching can benefit everyone. Since an employee who improves helps the manager, the department, the organization, and even coworkers, it makes sense to consider improvement as a shared responsibility.

Process. There are as many ways to diagnose performance and coaching as there are people. *The key point:* problem diagnosis and coaching occur throughout the year. They can be used as part of the appraisal process, but they also fit in whenever managers and employees communicate about performance (e.g., regular meetings during the year, staff meetings).

Result. Apart from producing solutions to prevent problems, the diagnostic and coaching processes can be documented for future reference, if there's a good reason to do so. For example, it's a good idea to keep track of coaching sessions to document the efforts a manager makes to improve a particular staff member's performance. Or, in diagnosing problems, you might generate work flowcharts or basic notes that might be useful in the future. In other cases, the diagnostic process could result in a written improvement action plan—a brief description of the problem and steps that need to be taken (when, by whom, how) to address it.

Back to Square One—Planning Again

After you do the annual performance review, coupled with the other parts of the system, you begin anew. Armed with the results from the discussion of last year's work, what went well and not so well, and why, you now incorporate that knowledge into the planning process for the next year.

Where Performance Management Fits into the Big Picture

To get the best possible return on performance management, link it to other processes in the organization. Performance management takes information from other processes and sends information to those other processes. What other processes?

Strategic Planning and Company Direction

Many companies have some means of looking to the future. Strategic planning at the corporate level can include a description of the general mission of the company, its values, and perhaps most important, its goals for the long term. That plan can then be translated into year-by-year plans that align with the longer-term strategic plan.

Where is the link to performance management? Both long- and short-term goals must be translated into goals and objectives for each smaller work unit and then into goals and objectives for each employee. That "translation" from company goals to individual responsibilities is done through the performance planning process we outlined earlier in the chapter. That process aligns the work of each employee with company purpose.

Beyond the alignment of purpose, the information collected from performance management can be used in the planning process. When you are planning, you are identifying barriers to success. Performance diagnosis provides that information. The more information you have about potential problems, the better you can avoid or overcome them.

Pay Levels, Rewards, and Promotions

Companies make decisions regarding pay levels, bonuses and other rewards, and promotions. An effective performance management system is helpful in making those decisions. If you don't base them on performance, you're likely to undermine your success.

Human Resource Development Planning

Human resource development planning is the fancy phrase for helping employees improve. In a constantly changing workplace, the skills needed for employee success change over time. Many companies take a proactive approach to help staff develop new skills by using performance management systems to identify gaps between what employees can do now and what they need to be able to do. Based on that information, which can be generated as part of the performance management process, companies can arrange for training, coaching, job shares and exchanges, formal education, and so on.

Budget Processes

Budgeting is a core process in any company. The budget for an organization often limits what employees can and can't

BE SURE YOU KNOW   **SMART**

Understand how managing performance fits in with other processes in your workplace. How can it be better integrated? How should performance man-   **MANAGING**
agement be influenced by budgets, planning, hiring? How should the results of performance management affect those other processes? Performance management takes input from other processes and informs or outputs to other processes.

do in carrying out their duties. Performance management is an ideal forum to ensure that all employees understand these constraints. Budgets provide input into performance management.

Performance management discussions can also provide information to assist in the budgeting process. For example, in performance planning, a manager and an employee identify a technological barrier to successful completion of a project. By identifying this in advance, they can budget additional funds to purchase new equipment so the project can be completed.

Manager's Checklist for Chapter 3

☑ Performance management is a system within a larger system. To get maximum benefit, you need to do the whole process, not a part of it.

☑ Performance management links up with strategic planning, budgeting, employee development, employee compensation systems, and quality improvement programs. The more links established between performance management and other processes in the organization, the better the return on investment.

Chapter
4

Getting Ready: Preparing to Start the Process

Where to start? First, gather the information you need to create meaningful, measurable goals with each staff member. Then lay the groundwork to work with employees.

Gathering Your Information

Since part of the power of performance management comes from helping the organization, its units, and its employees "pull in the same direction," the more information you and employees have about where the organization is going and how it's going to get there, the better you'll be able to link individual performance expectations to the success of the organization. This is also a first step toward raising the level of employee engagement by providing meaning and context for the work employees do.

What kinds of information will be helpful? Let's look at a list for the "big picture." The following can be useful in forging the links between *employee* purpose and *organization* purpose:

- the strategic plan of the company
- the one-year (short-term) operational plan of the company
- strategic and operational plans for the next-smallest subunit (e.g., division or department)
- the strategic and operational plan for your own work unit

For the "smaller picture," you may also need:

- job descriptions for each employee
- the performance appraisal information for each employee for the previous year

How will this information help, and how do you use it?

Strategic and Operational Plans

Where possible, get these plans in place prior to embarking on performance management. If any pieces are missing, and they often are, don't worry. Forge on. Flexibility is important.

SMART

MANAGING

MORE INFORMATION IS BETTER

The more "big picture" information you have, the better you'll be able to align individual job tasks with the needs of your unit and company. Some information might be unavailable when you need it. In that case you have to make the best of the situation. It shouldn't stop you from continuing.

Generally, a strategic plan sets out where the company is going over a certain period of years. It may explain the business of the company, its values and principles, and the goals it has set for the period. It may also include an analysis of the external factors that could affect the business (economy, demographics, etc.), a look at past performance to determine future targets, and an identification of the resources the company needs to achieve its long-term goals.

Strategic plans aren't for the company as a whole. Planning should cascade down—although that doesn't often happen. The top managers go through the strategic planning process for the company. The plan that results provides an umbrella under which the divisions or departments do their strategic planning. Then the strategic plan devised for each division or department provides an umbrella for the component units in the planning process.

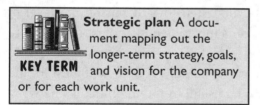

KEY TERM

Strategic plan A document mapping out the longer-term strategy, goals, and vision for the company or for each work unit.

This cascading of strategic planning is logical. Why? Because the purpose, roles, goals, and values of each unit should support or link up with the company's purpose, roles, goals, and values. If each unit achieves its strategic objectives, the company will have achieved its strategic objectives as well, because the objectives are linked.

Operational plans differ from strategic plans. Operational plans deal with a shorter time span, often one year. They can be more detailed, outlining what each work unit must accomplish in a year. Like strategic plans, operational plans can exist for the company as a whole, the larger subunits, and on down to the smallest work units. Each yearly operational plan needs to be consistent and take into account the larger strategic plans.

OK. So now you've got strategic plans and operational plans. What next? Let's look at a case study.

The Argon Company consists of three divisions: human resources, production, and sales. Within each of those divisions are several smaller units. In its strategic planning process, Argon executives ad-

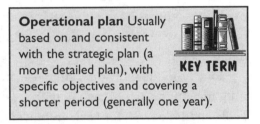

Operational plan Usually based on and consistent with the strategic plan (a more detailed plan), with **KEY TERM** specific objectives and covering a shorter period (generally one year).

dressed the concern that new competitors might grab a significant market share from Argon unless the company takes action over the next five years. The managers identified two strategic goals or objectives they felt were vital to stay in business:

1. Maintain or increase current market share over the next five years.
2. Increase profitability by reducing waste.

Based on these two strategic goals, the company, in its yearly operational plan, set two specific goals:

1. Maintain or increase current market share this year by identifying and recruiting new clients.
2. Reduce waste and faulty products by 5 percent this year.

The three divisions were expected to identify how they would contribute to these goals over the long term and the short term. They came up with strategies for doing so. For example, the human resources division created the following strategic objectives for the five-year period:

- Provide ongoing training in identifying causes of poor quality.
- Establish a reward system to encourage employees to identify potential clients.

. . . and the following operational objectives for the current year:

- Determine needs for training and development in discovering the causes of poor quality.
- Identify ways to deliver training in a cost-effective way.
- Examine hiring practices to determine whether more effective sales staff can be hired and retained.

The production and sales divisions established different objectives, of course, with the overall corporate goals dictating their objectives.

The process continued in a similar way with the smaller units. For example, within the human resources division, the training branch took on objectives involving training, while the personnel branch took on hiring, retaining, and rewarding.

Finally, in the individual employee performance management planning meetings, each branch manager set with his or her employees the goals and objectives for each employee so they reflected the objectives of the branch. For example, the training branch manager assigned one employee to identify training needs and another to find cost-effective ways to deliver that training.

TRICKS OF THE TRADE

INVOLVE STAFF IN PLANNING

Regardless of what the rest of the company does, many managers find it useful to set aside one day a year to meet with staff and identify what the unit needs to accomplish in the coming year. This ensures that staff are on the same page, it's generally motivating and empowering, and it reduces the amount of "paper plans imposed from above." This approach works particularly well when there are no more than 20 people in the unit.

At Argon, each employee contributes to the goals of his or her branch, each branch contributes to the goals of the division, and each division does its share toward achieving the company goals. That's what we mean by integrating performance management into the big picture. That's why you need information about strategic and operational plans. This forms the basis for your employee goal-setting.

If Information Is Missing and Reality Intervenes

If you think the above process sounds like a big undertaking, you're correct. The truth is many managers in many companies don't know what they're trying to achieve or where they're going. They don't plan well, so when they hit the mark it's often by accident. Or, they don't plan in a timely way to support performance management with employees.

If you can't access this information, what then?

Imagine your company doesn't have a plan, either long or short term. Assume your division doesn't either. You can't *force* executives to develop strategic, operational, and division plans, but you can plan for your own unit.

If you've been working for the company for a while, you have some idea of what it needs to do to succeed. Use

SMALLER BUSINESSES

TRICKS OF THE TRADE

Although we've used a large company as an example, the cascade approach to planning applies to any business. You need to be flexible. If you manage a restaurant with a staff of seven, for example, you can still follow the same pattern, although you won't have so many documents to examine. Maybe none. So long as you know what the restaurant needs to do to succeed, short term and long term, you can link individual job roles to hit those targets.

what you know informally to determine what your unit needs to do over the next several year(s).

Some "Smaller Picture" Information

Apart from the big picture information we've described, you'll find two other things useful, if not essential.

You need a copy of the employee's last formal performance review and related documentation. Since the performance review and the performance planning meeting are often combined or take place around the same time, this won't be an issue.

Why do you need this information? Because if there were remaining performance issues from past years, you want to follow up.

You'll want job descriptions for every employee—if they exist and if they are up to date. What's a job description? It's a statement that outlines the responsibilities, job tasks, and levels of authority for a position. Often

DON'T WAIT FOREVER
You can never get the performance management process perfect. Since it's a people process, it doesn't have to be perfect. If information is missing, try to obtain it or at least to fill in any critical blanks. Don't wait for other parts of the organization to do it for you—or you may wait forever.

a job description is developed for hiring or to determine pay levels.

Job descriptions provide starting points for setting employee goals. If you've got good job descriptions, use the lists of responsibilities to generate specific objectives and expectations about what constitutes good performance for each job.

There's a problem, though. While many experts suggest using job descriptions to guide objective setting, many job descriptions are out of date. It's costly and time consuming for companies to update their job descriptions. Work changes so quickly that job descriptions can become outdated in a single year as responsibilities change. Employees often perform duties not in their job descriptions. So if you use a job description as a starting point, review and modify it—early on in the performance planning process—so it reflects what the employee does.

Understanding job drift. *Job drift* occurs over time as *people* evolve the functions they carry out. For example, let's say you manage three computer analysts who have identical job descriptions. Each person has unique strengths and weaknesses. Over time and in an informal way, what they really do on a day-to-day basis changes. Good managers harness employee strengths. One analyst is great at testing code, while another is better at writing system specifications, while yet another is a customer service and communications genius.

Of course, you'll assign work based on these strengths. It may end up that the job descriptions are the same, but the actual jobs *people* do are different.

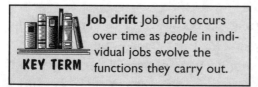

Job drift Job drift occurs over time as *people* in individual jobs evolve the functions they carry out.

KEY TERM

Is this a bad thing? No. We can't run successful organizations by job description. Individual employee goals should differ according to strengths and weaknesses and what employees actually do. The implication? Discuss with employees what they actually do, rather than what the job description says they do. It's essential to keep the entire process "real" and relevant.

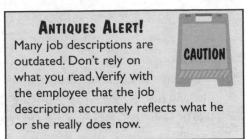

ANTIQUES ALERT!
Many job descriptions are outdated. Don't rely on what you read. Verify with the employee that the job description accurately reflects what he or she really does now.

Now that you've gathered the information or as much of it as possible, how else can you prepare for performance planning meetings?

Preparing and Educating Staff

For some reason, employees get overlooked in the performance management process. It's rare that companies and managers help them become proactive participants through preparing and educating them. Go figure.

If employees don't understand the process and how it benefits them, they'll worry about it. The greater the uncertainty, the more likely they'll enter into it with resistance, hostility, or anger. That puts you behind the eight ball when you're trying to develop a cooperative climate for the process.

You must prepare and educate your staff. Human resources departments can help. Policies can help, but not much. Your employees need to know what *you* are going to do with them, and that can vary from manager to manager. They need to hear it from you, and they need to hear it in person.

How to Prepare and Educate Staff

First, let's outline what staff need to know to work with you in the performance management process:

- why performance management is important (purpose)
- how it will benefit them, you, and the company
- your general philosophy or approach (e.g., working together, centered on self-evaluation, focus on prevention of performance problems)

They need to know what to expect at the initial meeting:

- What will happen during performance planning meetings?
- What kinds of input are they expected to supply?
- What kinds of questions will you ask them?
- How will decisions be made during the meetings?
- How flexible will the objectives and job tasks be?
- What kinds of preparation do they need to make?
- How long will the meetings take?

They'll also want to know details about the later parts of the process, particularly about the appraisal meeting:

- What will happen at the yearly review?
- How will disagreements be handled?
- How will the appraisals affect pay, bonuses, and so on?

Employees are sure to have a lot of questions and concerns. Consider holding a general staff meeting to explain the process. It should precede your performance planning meeting by a few weeks. Do this every year to explain the process to new hires, remind experienced employees, and keep everyone focused on what's important.

Let's bring this chapter to a close by looking at how one manager prepared staff before beginning individual meetings with them. Note the tone, the style, and the details.

> **CAUTION**
>
> **EMPLOYEE NEGATIVITY**
>
> Understand that many employees have had bad experiences with performance management and may react negatively to a new or unfamiliar system, even if that system will ultimately help them. Explain it as well as you can, but accept that some will be resistant. Even the best explanation is words; negative employees will need proof in action. When they see you act in cooperative ways to help them, then they will believe.

What Staff Preparation Looks Like

George manages a work unit of 18 people. Because of a flattening of the organization, all staff report directly to him (no supervisors). He's introducing a new performance management method. He's called a staff meeting to discuss the new way of doing things. This is what he says:

Over the last year we've changed a lot around here. Some of you have commented that you aren't getting enough guidance about your work and that sometimes you don't know what's important and what's less important. You've also commented on the rating system we've been using to evaluate performance, saying it hasn't been helpful. We're going to do things differently because we need to focus on helping each other succeed. We're all going to have a better idea of where we are going and what we need to do. This will also help us catch problems as they occur during the year.

Before I talk about the details, I know we've all been through changes before, where all that's changed is the words or the forms. I don't expect you to feel excited about these changes, at least until you've had a chance to experience them, and until I've had a chance to prove to you that this *is* different, and that it *is* going to be helpful.

We'll start our new performance management system in about two weeks. I'll set up meetings with each of you so we can discuss what's important about your job, how it fits with our bigger goals, and where and how you should focus your energies. We'll agree on some targets, which we'll use at the end of the year to evaluate the progress made by our unit and by each of you. We're doing this *together!* It's not something I will be doing to you.

After we set the objectives in our initial performance planning meetings, we'll set up ways to communicate with each other so I know what's going on with each of you throughout the year and can help you achieve your goals. After all, that's my job—to help you get your work done.

Since our first step is the meetings beginning in a few weeks, let's talk about what we'll be doing.

George explains the relationships among the company's goals, the branch's goals, and each person's individual goals.

In the meetings we're going to determine if your job description is accurate. We want to know how you can best contribute to the goals of the organization. Together, we'll set some targets for you. I'm going to ask you a

COMMUNICATE AND COMMUNICATE AGAIN

SMART MANAGING

It's easy for people to misunderstand or forget. It's always a good idea to provide a written summary of key points. Keep it short.

SELL THE NEW WAY

When introducing a performance management system, stress the benefits for everyone, including employees. There are many, including clearer understanding of priorities, more decision-making power, less need to consult the manager, knowing where you stand throughout the year, no surprises.

Managers commonly make the mistake of focusing on why the system is good for the company. Staff need to know how it will be good for them.

lot of questions, because each of you is the expert at your job. Here are some things I'll ask:

- Is your job description accurate? What needs to be updated?
- How do you see yourself best contributing to the goals of our work unit?
- What's the best way to measure contributions at the end of the year?
- How can I help you hit your targets/goals? What do you need from me?
- What barriers do you see as affecting your job performance? How can we overcome them?
- What authority levels do you need to do your job?
- What are the most important parts of your job?

I'd like you to think about these questions before we meet. That will save us time. Jot down some notes between now and when we meet.

At the end of our meeting, both of us should know what you need to do and how we'll review your performance at the end of the year. We'll document this so we can refresh our memories throughout the year.

That's where we're going to start. Let me explain how we'll use that information throughout the year and at the end of the year, and how this is going to help all of us.

George provides more information, then concludes:

To summarize, I'll be setting individual meetings with you, about an hour apiece. Between now and the meeting, review your job descriptions, review the objectives our unit is expected to reach this year, and read the short version of our overall company plan. Also think about the questions I'm going to ask you and make some notes.

I know this is new to all of us and we'll be feeling around a bit. You probably have a lot of questions. You can ask them now or, if you prefer, you can pop in over the next few days with your concerns.

George opens the floor for questions.

Manager's Checklist for Chapter 4

☑ Preparing for the performance planning meeting is critical to paving the way for a more comfortable process where parties will feel at ease.

☑ Identify documentation or material you'll need at the meetings. Make sure employees have what they need beforehand (i.e., job descriptions, last year's performance review) and have time to review it.

☑ Don't rely on job descriptions because they are often outdated or don't reflect what employees do because of job drift. Remember, you are planning for *people*, not positions.

☑ If you're doing things a new way, communicate, communicate, communicate. Explain the details, explain the benefits, and explain the point. Provide a written summary of the process. The more employees understand, the easier the process will be, the more you'll be able to work *with* staff, and the less anxiety will be created.

☑ To save time, staff can do some premeeting work to address the questions you'll be asking them. Explain why this prework is important and how it will save time.

Performance Planning: Setting Targets

Too many people believe that *appraisal* is the most important part of performance management. They are mistaken. *Planning* is more important because it's forward looking, while appraisal looks in the rearview mirror.

Real increases in productivity come from aiming the employee at the bull's-eye, and then getting out of the way.

Let's define *performance planning*. It's a process by which employee and manager work together to determine what the employee should be doing in the next year and what successful performance means.

Other important parts of performance planning discussions are:

- identifying assistance the manager will provide
- identifying potential barriers to achievement and how to overcome them
- job tasks (priorities) and levels of authority

Some Issues

In this chapter, we address two issues: the people side of performance planning and the nuts and bolts of the process for setting objectives and standards. Before we do that, we have to consider a few things.

We use a modified version of "management by objectives (MBO)" sometimes called "management by results." While many books on MBO or

Performance planning
KEY TERM The process by which the employee and manager work together to plan what the employee should do in the upcoming year, define how performance should be measured, identify and plan to overcome barriers, all while creating a common understanding about the job.

management by results stress the importance of technical skills involved in performance planning, we don't do that. If you need to know all about goals, objectives, results, key result areas, standards of performance, engineered standards, objective standards, subjective standards, and so on, there are other resources available.

If you create a *common understanding* between manager and employee, it doesn't matter whether you know the technical terms. If you want to learn the definitions, that's fine, but you don't need them to succeed. Managers are often defeated and overwhelmed by all the jargon, so let's make it as simple and practical as possible.

We also need to talk about perfection—about writing "perfect" objectives or standards. Too many managers waste time trying to get them perfect, to make them perfectly measurable or perfectly objective (no subjectivity allowed). This attempt at perfection discourages people from carrying out the process as they pursue the impossible.

Keep the following in mind: The less important the job task, the easier it is to measure it precisely and objectively. The more important the task (and the more complex), the more difficult it is to measure. For example, you can measure the number of rings it takes for an employee to answer phone calls. That's easy. How do you measure the quality of service the employee offers while on the phone? It's more difficult to do that, because the task is more complex—and more important. So, put aside the myth that it's possible to measure everything in an exact and meaningful way.

SMART
AVOID THE SEARCH FOR PERFECTION
MANAGING Objectives and standards are never "objective." If you try to be "technically correct," you risk making the process frustrating and difficult. Perfection paralysis is an insidious disease. Focus on creating common understanding. Save the search for perfection for management consultants and researchers.

An Overview of the Performance Planning Process

Performance planning involves face-to-face meetings and work done independently by manager and employee. We outline the overall process, paying special attention to the face-to-face part of the process, the performance planning meeting(s). That's where the people process lives.

Purpose and Outcomes

The purpose of the performance planning process can best be defined in terms of the outcomes. By the conclusion of the performance planning process:

- The job tasks and objectives of the employee will be aligned with the goals and objectives of the work unit and the company. The employee will understand the link between his or her responsibilities and the overall goals.
- Job descriptions and job responsibilities will be modified to reflect changes in the work context.
- Manager and employee will agree on the major job tasks for the employee, how success will be measured, what job tasks are most important and least important, and the level of authority the employee will have with respect to each job responsibility.
- Manager and employee will identify any help the manager can provide, any potential barriers to achieving the objectives, and means of overcoming the barriers.
- A formal document (a performance plan) will be produced that summarizes the discussions and agreements and is signed by both manager and employee.

The Process/Steps

We can divide performance planning into three major phases: preparing, meeting, and finalizing the process.

First, preparing—beginning the linking of individual objectives to organizational needs. Both manager and employee have to be familiar with where the organization is going. This can be done before they meet. Also, the employee can review the job description independently. The preparation phase can involve manager, employee, or both, in reviewing:

- the company's strategic or operational plans (or goals)
- the work unit's plans or goals and objectives
- the last performance appraisal and/or performance plan
- the employee's current job description

The second phase, the heart of performance planning, is the meeting. Manager and employee sit down, usually in private, to discuss work for the next year. Here are the principles you'll apply.

- Since the employee is usually the most familiar with his or her job, the planning process involves a relatively equal partnership between manager and employee. They negotiate, because they share a common interest—success.
- Because the employee is an expert in the job, it's the employee who should generate the criteria used to gauge success, with the manager's involvement.
- The manager may be more expert in the "big picture" issues and how the employee fits with other employees and the needs of the work unit and organization. That's the major contribution on the manager's part.
- Because the manager initiates performance planning, it's the manager's job to create a climate for real dialogue and teamwork during the meeting.

Last, there may be a final or review phase, where manager and employee tie up loose ends or sign off on objectives and standards. This could be in the form of a shorter, follow-up meeting.

The Performance Planning Meeting

We're going to create a road map for the performance management meeting. Flexibility is key, but keep in mind the principles above. Since we're focusing on the people side, we provide examples of dialogue for each part of the meeting.

Let's introduce you to the two people involved in our example. Neil is a management consultant and instructional designer in a flexible, ever-changing work environment. Sharlene is Neil's manager. Neil and Sharlene meet for performance planning about two weeks after they reviewed

Neil's performance for last year and about a month after all the staff met to discuss goals and objectives for the entire work unit.

Climate Setting and Focusing

In setting the climate and direction, focus on the reasons for meeting and what the outcomes should be. Create a climate where both parties have some level of comfort for frank, constructive discussion. The manager is responsible for kicking off the process. How does Sharlene do it with Neil?

Before Neil arrived, Sharlene arranged for coffee to be available in the office and made sure she had copies of Neil's job description, his last performance review, and information about the work unit's objectives for the coming year. She placed a high priority on the meeting, so only an emergency could cause its cancellation, and she made sure nobody would interrupt during the meeting.

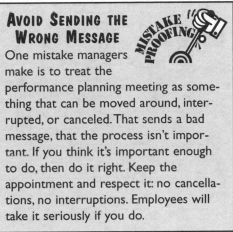

AVOID SENDING THE WRONG MESSAGE

One mistake managers make is to treat the performance planning meeting as something that can be moved around, interrupted, or canceled. That sends a bad message, that the process isn't important. If you think it's important enough to do, then do it right. Keep the appointment and respect it: no cancellations, no interruptions. Employees will take it seriously if you do.

When Neil arrived, she offered him a cup of coffee and they chatted for a minute or two. Then Sharlene focused the meeting.

She said: "Neil, this is the third year you and I have done this, so I imagine I don't need to give you a long explanation of what we're going to do. But let me do a quick review. Our task is to come to a common understanding about your job responsibilities, what you should be doing, and how we can measure success. This is also a chance to talk about what I can do to help you and a chance for you to clarify anything you want to talk about with respect to the job or our work unit. Before we get started, are there issues or questions we need to talk about?"

Neil replied: "Something's been bugging me about teamwork, and I would like to talk about it today. Now that we're moving to a team environment, I've got some questions about what that's going to mean to me

TRICKS OF THE TRADE

FOCUS FAST AND THEN INTERACT

It's important to involve the employee early in the meeting. If you give a detailed explanation of the planning meeting to all staff earlier in the week, all you need to begin each meeting is a few words to set the focus. Then start the interaction.

SMART MANAGING

MAXIMIZING MEETING TIME

Make the most of your meeting time by focusing on the communication part, the people part of the meeting. The better prepared you are, the more you can focus on communication and shared understanding.

as management consultant and instructional designer. I'm not sure how I can best contribute to our team or what you expect from me."

Sharlene replied: "Good question. Let's come back to that. You know, maybe that's something I should discuss with all the staff. I hadn't thought of that."

Reviewing Relevant Information

Before manager and employee can talk about specific job responsibilities, both need a shared understanding of what the work unit needs and where it's going. Other information that provides a context and meaning for their discussion of specific job responsibilities can also be shared.

This is how Sharlene started the process. "You were at our branch planning meeting, so you know what we need to do to help the company meet its goals. You recall we talked about contributing to accident reduction, helping to lower sick leave . . . "

Sharlene summarized the main points. Then she asked, "Given these targets, where do you see yourself fitting into the work unit plan?"

Neil jumped in: "I know the data we reviewed at the branch planning meeting suggested we might need to beef up our workplace health and safety training, but we aren't sure what that would look like. As instructional designer, the job of determining what we need rests with me, as should the design of any programs we decide on. There are other areas where I might fit, for example, in the areas of stress management consulting and training, and safety audits, since I have some experience in those areas."

Sharlene replied, "That's close to my thinking, but I want to make sure that you don't get overloaded. The company has set some brutal deadlines. But that's a good start. We'll come back to that. I have a few more questions to ask about your job description."

Sharlene pulled out a copy of Neil's job description. "The personnel office has asked us to review job descriptions. Here are your major responsibilities and the amount of

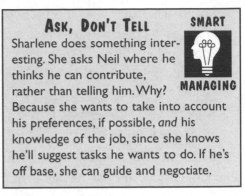

ASK, DON'T TELL SMART

Sharlene does something interesting. She asks Neil where he thinks he can contribute, rather than telling him. Why? MANAGING

Because she wants to take into account his preferences, if possible, *and* his knowledge of the job, since she knows he'll suggest tasks he wants to do. If he's off base, she can guide and negotiate.

time you're expected to spend on course design, consulting, and so on. Given what you know, and taking into account what you did last year, do these figures make sense or do we need to adjust them?"

Neil said he thought the time he spent on course design had increased, from 20 to 50 percent. He suggested modifying the job description to reflect that increase and the current needs of the unit. After a brief discussion, both agreed.

Sharlene summarized, "We've agreed you can best contribute over the next year by bumping up your course design time to half-time. That certainly reflects unit needs. I think we also agree that your role is critical in the areas of accident prevention, identifying how we might go about that, and perhaps additional course design. Are we on the same wavelength so far?"

Getting Specific: Job Responsibilities and Objectives

So far the discussion has been general. Now it gets specific. Once you have general job responsibilities, it's time to move on to writing specific objectives. An *objective* is a statement of a specific result or outcome the employee is expected to create or contribute to. Objectives can also include time or resource constraints (e.g., "by February 6" or "within allocated budget"). Here are some pointers on setting objectives:

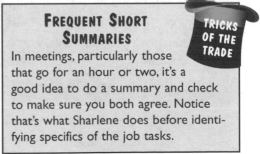

FREQUENT SHORT SUMMARIES TRICKS OF THE TRADE

In meetings, particularly those that go for an hour or two, it's a good idea to do a summary and check to make sure you both agree. Notice that's what Sharlene does before identifying specifics of the job tasks.

- Make each objective as specific as possible.
- Focus each objective on a single job responsibility or outcome.
- Specify when the result should occur and any limits on resources.
- Keep the objectives short, to the point, and direct.
- Focus the objectives on results or outcomes, not on how the employee is to achieve the results, except when there's a process the employee must follow.

Both employee and manager must understand the meaning of the objective in the same way. It should also make sense to others who read the document. Here are examples of specific objectives:

- Catalog the library collection completely by January 28, within the $10,000 budget.
- Respond to customer requests for information about products.
- By the end of the year, reduce customer wait time by 15 percent.
- Without raising staff levels, increase departmental sales by 5 percent.

Let's return to Sharlene and Neil.

Sharlene summed up their discussion of Neil's responsibilities. "You have in your job description four basic responsibilities: course design, consulting directly with managers, course delivery, and supporting your teammates on projects where they need your help. Let's go through those one by one and see if we can set some specific objectives."

Neil was ready and jumped in, "Sure. Under 'course design' ... We can't design courses without doing proper data analysis and needs assessment, to make sure the solutions we provide address the safety problems. Any objective has to cover that, to do it right."

Sharlene replied: "OK. Let's write an objective to cover analysis and assessment. Want to take a shot?"

Neil thought about it and said, "How about this? Under 'course design,' we put 'Write a plan to reduce accidents and lower sick leave (by June 30), following the basic processes and standards agreed to by the branch.'"

"Sounds pretty good," Sharlene observed. "I guess that end bit means you'll be doing interviews, needs assessments, and the other things in our standard process document?"

"Yes, exactly," Neil said. "But that's not the whole thing. We need a strategy, so we need another objective about implementing the strategy."

Neil and Sharlene contin-
ued the process for each
major job responsibility area
for Neil's position. Here are a
few more objectives they
agreed on:

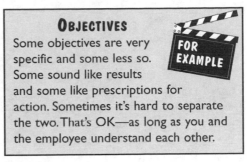

OBJECTIVES

Some objectives are very specific and some less so. Some sound like results and some like prescriptions for action. Sometimes it's hard to separate the two. That's OK—as long as you and the employee understand each other.

■ Within budget and consistent with the plan, design
and deliver necessary training courses (number to be determined)
and evaluate their effectiveness by December 31.

■ Carry out safety audits in a timely manner for managers and departments requesting them.

■ Provide assistance (on request) to Phil, Marie, and Joe on the X, Y, and
Z projects.

Developing Criteria for Success (Setting Standards)

Now comes the tough part. We need a way to determine if the employee
has attained the goals and objectives. We need performance standards.

Performance standards are statements that outline what criteria will
be used to determine if the employee has met each objective. They
answer such performance questions as "When?" "How good?" "How few
errors?" and "To whose satisfaction?" Generally standards should be:

■ specific
■ attainable with effort and "stretching"
■ as objective and measurable as possible

You may find that if the objectives you write are very specific, the
standards will be almost identical. Don't worry about getting everything
perfect. The point is having a shared understanding.

Sharlene opened the transition from objectives to standards. "We
have a good idea of what you need to be doing. How are we going to
determine at the end of the year if you've succeeded? Let's start with the
workplace safety and health objectives. What do you think would be a
good measure or standard?"

Neil thought for a moment. He answered, "Isn't the bottom line low-
ering the accident rate? If what I do doesn't contribute to that, then we

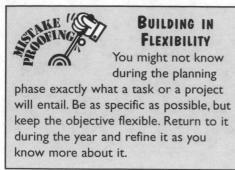

BUILDING IN FLEXIBILITY
You might not know during the planning phase exactly what a task or a project will entail. Be as specific as possible, but keep the objective flexible. Return to it during the year and refine it as you know more about it.

can't really call it a success. How about a standard like "Objective will be met if accident rate falls by X percent in 2013"?

Sharlene frowned, then asked, "Neil, are you sure you want to do that? You know one of the things about setting standards is that if you're going to be evaluated on something, you should be in control of it. I don't see how you can be in control of accidents for the entire plant."

Neil responded: "Well, what's going to happen if I don't meet whatever standard we set?"

Sharlene laughed because she sensed Neil was kidding. "Well, I can't see us firing you. But it is important. If we set a standard like that and you don't meet it, we would sit down to determine why it didn't happen, where we went wrong, and how we can fix it. Basically we would have to do a diagnosis, but it wouldn't be like sticking you with the blame for things beyond your control."

Neil came back with: "I like a challenge. We should measure this by the results we want. I can live with that standard."

Sharlene ended the discussion by agreeing, but she asked Neil to think about the reduction target, taking into account his lack of control. They agreed to finalize that standard next week. Sharlene moved on to another objective.

"Let's consider a standard for the safety audit objective. How will we know whether you've achieved that objective?"

Neil replied, "We don't want managers waiting six months for me to do the audit. Let's talk about turnaround time and customer satisfaction."

They agreed on this standard: "Objective will be achieved if requested safety audits are completed within four weeks of the request and are considered satisfactory (no complaints) by managers involved."

Neil and Sharlene went through a similar process to set standards for the other objectives. Finally they got to the following objective: "Provide support to other staff members on projects in relevant areas of expertise."

Sharlene asked, "How do we assess that one?"

Neil thought for a moment. "You said we needed to have objective measures if possible. We could count the number of meetings I have on those projects with Phil, Marie, and Joe, or the time I spend with each of them. We could measure that. Or, we could say that if their projects succeed, I've done my job."

"I don't like any of those," Sharlene replied. "Do we care how many meetings you have? Let's ask Phil, Marie, and Joe what kind of help you can provide and see if they can set some standards for you. After all, your job is to help them with what they need—they're your 'customers.' I'll set up a meeting tomorrow to discuss it. That way we'll all be on the same wavelength."

Discussion of Barriers and Help Needed

Once manager and employee set the standards, there are still a few things to deal with. Remember that our goal is to prevent problems getting in the way of goal attainment, so the next step is to discuss any difficulties, challenges, or problems that might interfere with achieving the objectives and meeting the standards. Managers can lead that discussion and add their views.

Sharlene began, "What kinds of obstacles do you see slowing you down? Is there anything I can do to help?"

Neil replied. "I expect there may be some resistance from the plant managers. After all, this is going to take some of their time. It would help if we could be sure that the 'higher-ups' make it a high priority and communicate that to the other managers."

Sharlene offered to talk to the CEO and vice president in charge to enlist their support. The conversation continued until they had discussed each of the objectives and standards, and Sharlene had a list of things she could do to help Neil.

> **INTEGRATING TEAM ISSUES**   *TRICKS OF THE TRADE*
>
> Some suggest that standards of performance overstress the individual's performance at the expense of team performance. Notice what Sharlene did to avoid this. Because part of Neil's role is to help members of the team, she decided to involve them in defining what that means.

Discussion of Priorities and Authorities

We're close to the end of the meeting. Two matters remain.

First, manager and employee must agree on which objectives are most important. This allows the employee to allocate his or her time without having to consult the manager. A simple way to do this is to designate a priority for each task or objective. For example, you might rate them as priority 1—essential, priority 2—important, and priority 3—least important.

Setting priorities is a straightforward process. Remember, employee and manager should do it together, so they arrive at a common understanding and the priorities reflect the needs of the work unit and the company.

The second matter to discuss is authority. Employees need to know when they can make decisions on their own and when they need to consult the manager. For each objective, discuss the level of decision making available to the employee. You can use the following rating system:

- Complete Authority: no need to get permission or report afterward
- Act and Then Report: can make decision and act, but needs to report decision to manager
- Ask: needs to get decision or permission to decide from manager

Levels of authority are affected by the ability and track record of the employee, the importance and nature of the decisions involved, and what the employee needs to do the job efficiently and effectively.

Ending the Meeting

The end of the meeting is important. It's a time to thank the employee, talk about how productive and useful the meeting has been, summarize key points, arrange to document the details of the discussion, and plan to tie up loose ends. This is how Sharlene handled it:

"This was hard work, but I think we are set for the year. Thank you. You wanted to discuss how you can contribute to the team. I think your revised job description and the objectives we've set show how important you are to our team and how you can contribute.

"Let's summarize. We both have our notes from this meeting. I'd like you to organize them and have a list of job task areas, objectives, and standards ready for next week. We'll also talk to Phil, Marie, and Joe to finish setting the standards that relate to them. I'm going to list the things I can do to help you and we'll attach that to your plan, so I don't forget. We should meet to make sure we've got everything, and then we can both sign your performance plan so it's clear we've developed it together. As we discussed, I'd like to talk to you every few months about your progress. We'll use the plan to guide those discussions."

The Follow-Up

More often than not, there's additional work after the planning meeting. In our example, Sharlene and Neil need to organize their notes, consult with other employees, and finalize some standards. Those things are best done after the meeting. There's another reason to have a follow-up meeting. Between the performance planning meeting and the follow-up, new ideas or issues may crop up, stimulated by the initial conversation. It's good to allow some time to reflect before finalizing the performance plan.

An Optional Step: Action Planning

Some managers add a step between the performance planning meeting and follow-up. They ask the employee to develop an action plan, a list of tasks or courses of action the employee intends to follow to achieve the objectives and meet the standards. At the follow-up meeting, the manager reviews the action plan with the employee. This makes it easier for the employee to provide status reports during the year, since he or she can use a checklist to update the manager. The disadvantage is that it's more paperwork and time. You need to decide for yourself whether action plans are a good idea.

Manager's Checklist for Chapter 5

☑ Throughout the performance management process, focus on the communication between you and the employee. If the two of you share an understanding, that's 90 percent of the job done.

☑ It's difficult to write excellent objectives and performance standards. Do your best by getting them as specific, objective, and measurable as you can without spending too much time.

☑ Your role in performance planning is to make decisions with the employee, help him or her understand what's important, and work together to set the objectives and standards.

☑ Make sure there's a process for documenting the agreements. Generally, the employee will assemble the final draft of the plan, and both employee and manager will sign off. If there are ways in which you will be helping the employee, attach your commitment to the plan.

Ongoing Performance Communication

What happens between planning and the performance review? Ongoing communication throughout the year. That's what makes performance management work. Yes, it's essential and no, it won't take up much of your time. Really.

Take out communication and it isn't performance management. It's planning and appraisal. Here's our definition:

Ongoing performance communication is the process by which manager and employee work together to share information about work progress, potential barriers and problems, possible solutions to problems, and how the manager can help the employee. It's the dialogue that links planning and appraisal.

The Purpose

Workplaces in the past tended to be pretty stable. People could do the same job over a year or period of years because the pace of change was slower.

That's no longer the case. The modern workplace is dynamic. The need to compete pushes companies to improve continuously. In general, the work is more complex and faster. Priorities change. Barriers spring up. Managers can't assume that staff will succeed if they simply maintain the set course. One purpose of *ongoing performance communication* is to

KEY TERM **Ongoing performance communication** The process by which manager and employee work together to share information about work progress, potential barriers and problems, possible solutions to problems, and how the manager can help the employee. Its importance lies in its power to identify and address difficulties before they grow.

keep the work process dynamic, flexible, and responsive. Communication can generate changes in objectives and job tasks and new or different priorities.

Communication helps us cope with changes, but even if there were no changes, we would need regular communication, because people need information. As a manager, you need certain information to coordinate the work of those reporting to you. You need to know the status of processes and projects so you can convey that information to your boss if necessary. You need to know whether things will be late or early. You need to avoid surprises. You need to identify potential and actual problems early enough so you can solve them before they become more difficult. Finally, to help staff do their jobs, you need information about how you can best help them.

Employees need information, too. What's changed in terms of their priorities? Has information come to the manager that's relevant to their performance, such as customer complaints or information about defects or product errors? Some staff need more feedback and support than others, but all employees need information about how they are doing to become and remain engaged and to improve.

In a nutshell, the purpose of ongoing performance communication is to make sure everybody has the information needed to improve throughout the year.

The Outcomes (Communication + Deliverables)

The details of ongoing performance communication are determined by what managers and employees need and want. Some managers want a paper trail to record progress, so they use simple forms to track it. Other managers want less paperwork, so they record only significant points that must not be forgotten.

The first step in determining what and how the communication will occur is to answer the following key questions:

INFORMATION AND EMPOWERMENT

Smart managers know the more informed their employees are about priorities, directions, and their job tasks, the less time managers will spend having to fight fires. Ongoing communication empowers employees to work and make decisions on their own.

- What information do I need from each employee to fulfill my responsibilities as a manager?
- What information does each employee need to fulfill his or her job responsibilities?

What kinds of questions need to be answered when you communicate about performance with employees?

- How are things going with respect to job responsibilities?
- What is going well? What is not going well?
- Is the employee on track to achieve objectives and meeting standards of performance?
- If things aren't on track, what needs to change to get things on track?
- How can the manager support improvement (even if everything is on track)?
- Has anything changed that might affect the employee's job tasks or priorities?
- If so, what changes need to be made in objectives and job tasks?

Formal Methods

There are two approaches to ongoing communication, one using formal methods, the other being less formal. You and your employees need to choose methods that work for you, but the idea is to minimize the time needed and not create more "overhead work."

Formal methods of communication are planned and scheduled. There are three methods:

1. regular written reports
2. regular manager-employee meetings
3. regular group or team meetings with the manager

Each method has advantages and disadvantages, so you get to choose the method that best suits your situation. You might even mix and match.

Regular Written Reports

Some managers benefit by having employees submit regular, written status reports. Unfortunately, many managers create huge amounts of paper and waste time this way, and it can drive employees crazy.

What are the advantages of written status reports? They don't require face-to-face meetings, so they are appropriate when employees and their manager are not in the same place.

MISTAKE PROOFING

AVOIDING OVERLOAD AND THE PAPER CHASE
Whether communicating in person or on paper, stay focused on what you need. A common problem in performance communication is to include too much.
For every thing discussed or reported, ask yourself, "How does this information help me or help the employee accomplish assigned job tasks?" If you have no answer, maybe there's no point in dealing with that particular bit of information. Don't collect useless information!

The disadvantages? The process can easily turn into a wasteful, pointless bureaucratic paper chase where nobody reads the reports. Few employees like doing them. Perhaps most important, written reports don't involve a dialogue. They're just a one-way flow of information from employee to manager. That problem can be overcome by combining various methods. For example, whenever a regular report contains red flags or problem indicators, the manager and employee can get together face-to-face or by phone for problem solving. Or, monthly reports can be supplemented by a face-to-face meeting every three months so the manager and each employee can discuss performance matters and so the manager can provide feedback and information to employees, one on one.

One more disadvantage of written reports and one-on-one meetings: both methods involve information sharing between only two people. What if you work in a team-based environment or a situation where it's important that a number of people share information? Neither method meets that communication need.

Options and formats. What gets reported in regular communication is up to you. What do you need? How often do you need it? Here are some options.

You can use a brief narrative. At specified intervals, each employee produces a short summary of progress, problems encountered, and the status of the major job tasks identified during the performance planning meetings. Most managers will provide some basic headings to structure the report. For example, Objective/Job Task, Status, Difficulties and Problems, and Improvement Ideas or Help Needed.

You can use a structured form with several columns. The form might include columns for employees to provide information on each of their objectives, job tasks, or standards. There might be a column for progress (on time, late, early), a column for problem identification, and so on. One advantage of a structured form? A master copy can be made for each employee, with the same objectives and job tasks listed on it. Each month, the employee simply fills in the columns on the form.

One final comment on written reports. Almost anything that can be put on paper can be transferred via e-mail. That technology can be particularly useful when employees and the manager are located at different sites.

Regular Manager-Employee Meetings

Written reports don't encourage the discussions and problem solving necessary to identify roadblocks early and to find and implement solutions. Regularly scheduled one-on-one meetings provide those opportunities. In addition to ensuring communication, face-to-face, regular meetings provide a sense of connection between manager and employee, something that can be motivating.

Disadvantages? They can be time-consuming, particularly if not structured well. They also require good interpersonal skills on the part of the manager so that communication is real, not only chitchat and cover-ups. But there are ways to overcome these disadvantages.

Here are some guidelines for regular status meetings:

■ Use your interpersonal skills to set the right tone for discussion and problem solving. (We provide tips for creating dialogue in the People Techniques section later in this chapter.)

- Meetings take people away from their work. Schedule ongoing communication meetings just often enough to help employees do their jobs.

> **TRICKS OF THE TRADE**
>
> ### MAKE MEETINGS MEANINGFUL
> One-on-one meetings are an essential part of communicating about performance. But people don't like meetings, unless they understand what's in it for them. Begin meetings by outlining (quickly), the purpose, and how the meeting will benefit them.

- People in certain jobs might need to meet more or less often than those in other jobs. Even people doing the same job may differ in terms of how much contact they need. You may want to handle the scheduling process on an individual basis.
- It isn't usually necessary to keep elaborate notes regarding progress meetings. Generally it's a good idea to record discussions about performance deficits, actions to be taken to resolve those difficulties, and discussions about outstanding performance. Documentation of these kinds of matters is useful at year-end reviews.

Conducting the One-on-One Meeting

There are many ways to conduct ongoing performance communication meetings. Regardless of how you go about it, keep in mind the purpose: to discuss and exchange information about job tasks so you and the employee can work together to improve. To give you a starting point, we've provided an outline of one way to conduct meetings.

Begin the meeting with a short *statement of purpose and focus*. For example: "We're here to discuss how your work is going, see if anything has changed since our last meeting, and see if there is anything that might help you carry out your job responsibilities."

Update the employee on changes you know about that may be relevant to his or her job. For example: "The board has decided on a change of direction that might affect our work. Let me explain."

Focus on specific job tasks and standards. For example: "Let's go through the objectives and standards we set in April. I'd like to know whether you feel you're on track to meet them, and if you've come up against any problems, and what we can do to fix them." While you'll focus on getting input, you may comment on problems you've noticed or compliment the employee on his or her work.

Problem solve as needed. If either of you feel something is off track, identify the reason(s) and work together to address the problem.

WHO TALKS MOST?   SMART

While status meetings should focus on dialogue, it's a good idea to have the employee do most of the talking. Encourage self-evaluation and reporting. Then you can comment or ask questions. If problems are identified, encourage the employee to suggest solutions.

MANAGING

Allow room for discussion of points that might be missed by focusing on specific tasks and objectives. For example: "Now that we've talked about your specific objectives, is there anything you feel I should know that would help me do my job better or make this place more effective?"

Record relevant information that might be needed later. You may want to share notes you take, particularly if they outline an agreement between the two of you.

Conclude with a summary and set a date for the next meeting. For example: "Good, now let's sum up. We've agreed you might benefit from XYZ training, so I will arrange that for you. At our next meeting in two months, we'll see whether things have gotten back on track with respect to those product defects we've discussed. Does that make sense?"

Group Meetings

The third formal method of communicating about performance occurs in a group setting. All group members meet regularly to update each other on the status of their work. Why do some workplaces use this approach? Isn't discussion of job performance something between each employee and the manager? Yes . . . and no.

Obviously some discussions ought to be held privately. Most routine communication about work can be shared among the employees. You have to decide.

Here's the argument. No employee is an island. Most jobs are interconnected, in some sort of system, so the work and tasks of one employee interact with the work and tasks of other employees. Employees can benefit from knowing and understanding what others are doing and from participating in the joint problem-solving efforts that are often necessary.

DISCIPLINE IN PRIVATE

CAUTION

When serious problems surface with respect to an individual's performance, a public forum is almost always the worst place to discuss them. Disciplinary action should take place in private, period. Bottom line: never do anything in a group meeting that will humiliate an employee.

What about disadvantages? Two stand out: time and trouble. Time spent in meetings may be a good investment, but it's still time taken away from other tasks. Some people hate meetings with a passion: they'll find reasons for missing them, which means more work for you. For small teams and groups, both disadvantages can be addressed by applying basic meeting management techniques and focusing on the purpose of update meetings.

Conducting the Group Status Meeting

Set the focus of the meeting. Review the purpose of the meeting. For example: "We've set aside 30 minutes to update each other on our objectives, tasks, and projects. If we identify things that need to be discussed at length, we can figure out how best to do that as we go."

Each person updates. Go around the room so each person reports on significant issues, progress, and difficulties. To structure the process, whoever is chairing the meeting can use standard questions. For example:

- Can you give us a brief update on how things are going with your job responsibilities?
- What is going well?
- What kinds of challenges or problems have occurred since the last meeting?
- Is there anything we can do to help?

Problem solve. If issues or problems are identified and can be dealt with quickly, do so. If not, establish a procedure to deal with the situation. You may want to schedule a smaller group meeting or ask somebody to develop a proposal.

Summarize and close. After each person has spoken and the group has identified and addressed any problems or issues, close with a summary of agreements made. For example: "John and Mary are going to work out a process so engineers and receptionists can coordinate their work better. They'll get back to us at our meeting next month. If anyone has suggestions, please pass them on to either of them."

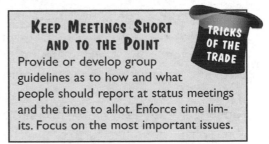

KEEP MEETINGS SHORT AND TO THE POINT
Provide or develop group guidelines as to how and what people should report at status meetings and the time to allot. Enforce time limits. Focus on the most important issues.

Finally, it's always a good idea to produce a summary (minutes) of meetings. Meeting participants can take turns doing that. The minutes serve as documentation, if needed later, and as a way to refresh memories.

Informal Methods

Not all ongoing communication between manager and employees is scheduled or formalized into meetings or on paper. In fact, there's a lot of benefit to informal meetings, chats, talking during coffee breaks, or the famous "management by walking around." At one organization the staff claimed they got more done in a 20-minute coffee break discussion with the boss present than at any of the lengthy scheduled meetings.

The advantage of using and promoting informal methods is they are "just in time." A problem or issue occurs. A brief conversation ensues right away and things can be set straight quickly. Since problems don't occur neatly the day before scheduled meetings, you must have other ways to communicate when scheduled meetings aren't soon enough.

With informal processes, there are no "correct" ways. Some managers allocate a certain part of their day or week to dropping in on staff and asking basic questions like,

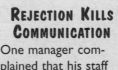

REJECTION KILLS COMMUNICATION
One manager complained that his staff never told him things he should know, despite his proclamation of an open-door policy. He didn't realize the problem was his attitude. When an employee approached him, he sometimes showed disinterest or even annoyance at being interrupted. So people stopped talking to him.

If you want staff to talk to you, make sure you receive visitors positively and make time for them.

How's everything going? or, Is there anything I can do to help you with
. . . ? or even, Hey, you sure handled that customer well!

One more thing. Walking around and talking informally is a good
method if done with skill and sensitivity. (More on that in a moment.)
What might be more important is setting a climate where employees feel
comfortable coming to you when things come up. That means being clear
about when you would like to be involved or consulted and making time
for employees who feel a need to discuss something.

People Techniques

Despite the best of intentions, managers can create situations where
their approaches to performance communication have negative effects.
In some cases, employees feel as if the boss is interrogating them. Or
they feel that being honest results in punishment or blame or more
work. Below are a few "people techniques" to avoid negative effects with
staff, regardless of communication format.

- Focus communication on *we*: How can we solve this problem? How
  can we make this easier? Or better still, How can I help?
- Don't use questions to intimidate or bully. Use questions to get
  enough information on the table so you and the employee can solve
  the problem.
- Make sure employees understand what you need, what you want,
  and what to expect so they can prepare for you. Don't assume that it's
  obvious.
- Don't look only at *problems*, but also at *successes*. People need to
  know what they're doing right, not only what they are doing wrong.
  Celebrate successes as they occur.
- Encourage staff to evaluate their own progress and work. They know
  what's going on, because they're closer than you to the work. On occa-
  sion you may have to guide staff to a more accurate assessment, but
  generally most employees will be honest if they understand that you
  want to help them succeed, rather than to find fault.

Communication in Action

Let's close this chapter with a description of how one manager went about the ongoing communication process. First, an important point. It has probably occurred to you that the best way to ensure communication about performance is by using several methods. Sometimes written reports might fit, but not only written reports. Regular individual meetings are good, but

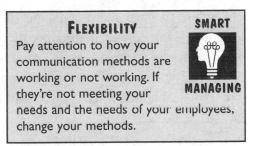

FLEXIBILITY

SMART MANAGING

Pay attention to how your communication methods are working or not working. If they're not meeting your needs and the needs of your employees, change your methods.

informal "just in time" conversations are important. Group or team meetings might work, but only if augmented by other techniques.

Sharon, as branch director, directly supervised 15 people. When she was promoted to the job, she continued two existing, formal methods for communicating with employees. First, each staff member was asked to complete a monthly update/status form and return it to her. Second, she met with each employee for about 10 minutes each month to discuss his or her report. She also had a knack for establishing good rapport with staff and did a good deal of informal communication.

This worked for the first six months, but then the organization got busier. Getting the written reports was like pulling teeth, and each month about half of them were late. She cajoled and threatened, but the reports continued to lapse.

Then Sharon did something interesting. She thought about her initial belief that everything should be documented monthly. And she thought about the delays and difficulties in making the reports method work. She wondered, "What is this telling me about what my employees need from me?" Her answer was that staff didn't find the process useful and considered it a waste of time. It had "negative value," at least to employees, and that's why it didn't work. Still, she felt she needed information regularly. Here's what she decided to do.

Sharon did away with the monthly written reports and meetings. Instead, she talked informally with people over coffee or walked around and visited them. That allowed her to stay in touch with her staff on a regular basis. She also set up short weekly staff meetings (just before the workday began) with a single purpose—to identify issues that needed immediate attention. Those meetings helped her to "red flag" potential problems early on.

Finally, she recognized that many issues required the involvement of a number of people in the organization. She established general staff meetings for that purpose, usually at the end of every second month.

The results were positive. The new approach esliminated a lot of paperwork. When Sharon needed to document something, perhaps a success or

SMART

MANAGING

USE MULTIPLE APPROACHES

Don't rely on a single communication approach. All have advantages and disadvantages. Use a combination of methods that meet both your needs and those of your staff.

a particular problem, she wrote basic notes. By using a combination of methods and by showing that she was working with the staff, she created a situation where she got better, more timely information when she needed it, while reducing unnecessary work.

Manager's Checklist for Chapter 6

☑ Choose the best combination of methods for communicating about performance. Begin by answering these two questions: What information do I need to do my job and when do I need it? and What information do my employees need to do their jobs and when do they need it?

☑ To promote an open, nonthreatening climate, explain the reasons for ongoing communication about performance and invite staff to suggest useful and efficient ways to do it.

☑ Aim all communication at identifying and solving problems, not blaming.

☑ Ongoing performance communication is a dynamic process. Modify your methods according to your situations—and your results. Customize to meet the needs of each employee.

☑ As with all the components of performance management, employees must perceive value for themselves. If they don't, it won't work. Listen to employees when they talk, and pay attention to what they do. There's a lot of information there.

Data Gathering, Observing, and Documenting

Performance management is a problem-solving and prevention process. Does it make sense to go by gut feeling? Are you prepared to discipline employees or give pay raises because you just feel it's deserved? When working with employees to help them improve, does it make sense to send them to a dozen training courses in the hope that something might work? If that's the best you can do, you'll waste resources—and won't improve performance.

For all these decisions, you need data and you need a way to record it and the decisions you make. That's our topic in this chapter.

Data gathering is an organized, systematic way to collect information about the performance of an employee, the work unit, or the organization. For example, you might have customers complete brief feedback forms, or you might count the number of widgets produced that need to be redone or fixed before they are shipped. You might look at turnaround time, the time required to process orders, or a multitude of other factors.

Observation is a special kind of data gathering. It's what you see or hear directly. If you hear an employee being rude to a customer, that's observation. If someone tells you an employee was mean to a customer, that's not observation, because you didn't see it or hear it yourself. When we talk about reasons for gathering information and observing, you'll see why this distinction is important.

Data gathering An organized, systematic way to collect information about performance, generally by measuring something.

KEY TERMS **Observation** A special kind of data gathering, when a manager sees or hears something directly, not from somebody else.

Finally, *documentation* refers to the actions a manager takes to record and keep track of data gathering, observations, and communication and decisions involving individual employees.

Why Do We Gather Data and Observe?

You don't have time to collect data for the fun of it. Nobody does. If you spend your time hovering over staff, watching them work, they get mighty tired of feeling as if there's a buzzard circling. Not to mention you probably have other things to do. So, let's look at why you need data and why you might need to observe staff.

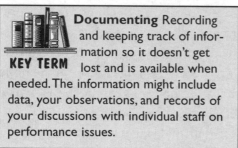

Documenting Recording and keeping track of information so it doesn't get **KEY TERM** lost and is available when needed. The information might include data, your observations, and records of your discussions with individual staff on performance issues.

We collect data and observe performance to identify and solve problems. To solve a problem, we need to know two things—that a problem exists and the cause of the problem. Sometimes, to convince someone that there's a problem, you need hard information, information that goes beyond the "maybe, sometimes, it's possible you could be doing better" approach.

There's another reason to collect data. If you have data to support your personnel decisions, you are less likely to become a target for lawsuits resulting from those decisions. If a complaint or lawsuit is launched you will have supporting documents to show you stayed on the right side of the law.

Reasons for Data Gathering, Observing, and Documenting

We can summarize the main reasons for data gathering, observing, and documenting as follows:

- Provide an ongoing, fact-based record of both positives and negatives of employee performance that can be used to make decisions.

- Identify potential problems as early as possible so they can be addressed and the employee can improve.
- Identify employee strengths so they can be developed further and then deployed most effectively.
- Enhance employee motivation and engagement through recognition of good work.
- Collect enough accurate information to prevent and solve problems.
- Record specifics of performance and communication about performance, to be used in disciplinary actions and related grievances or potential legal complaints.

What Do We Gather? What Do We Document?

You could become a data junkie, picking up information and recording it like a manic stamp collector. That's not wise. Data collection takes time, effort, and money. The more data you collect, the more resources you need to make sense of it, to use it. Making sense of data isn't a trivial process.

What you gather will depend in part on the goals and objectives of your organization. If your unit provides a service to customers, gathering customer satisfaction information is useful. Although we can't tell you what data will be useful, we can offer some suggestions.

We focus mostly on information related to performance management. But keep in mind that performance management is only a part of the continuous improvement process. Consider gathering information for the following purposes:

- To determine instances of great or poor performance (e.g., widgets produced by each worker, number of faulty widgets, customer complaints, customer praise).
- To identify the causes of performance problems. (Do employees have trouble making only certain widgets? Or only when they have to work quickly? Do they receive customer complaints only when under stress? From women? From men?)
- To ascertain the factors behind excellent performance (managers never seem to think about that purpose!). By finding out how your best employees work, you can use that information to help others improve. Benchmark your best performers.

- To provide evidence to determine whether your employees have achieved their objectives and standards. Data you collect is determined by the standards you set with staff.

Where do you get the information? Again, it depends on what you need. But information can come from many sources:

- Direct customers
- Executives
- Employees
- Yourself (manager)
- Employees and managers in other departments in your company who interact with your department and employees
- Suppliers

The next question is: what do I document? With respect to performance management itself, you're probably going to document or track:

- achievement (of lack of achievement) of objectives and standards
- praise and critical comments received about an employee's behavior or work
- specific evidence needed to substantiate either inferior work or superior work
- other data that will help you and employees identify causes of problems (or successes)
- records of performance-related conversations you have with an employee, which you should have the employee sign if the issue is serious
- critical incident data

That last item, *critical incident data*, refers to extreme behavior—usually negative, such as arriving at work drunk, swearing at a customer, yelling, harassing fellow employees, or theft. As you can imagine, some critical incidents might be grounds for immediate dismissal.

When these incidents occur, it's best to record as much information as possible, as soon as possible. For example, consider the employee who arrives at work smelling of liquor and slurring words. You should record date, time of contact, discussions that ensued at that time, details of employee behavior, and how the incident was handled. The report can be written as a little narrative, a story about the event. As they used to say on *Dragnet,* "Just the facts." Describe what happened as best you can. Don't embellish or interpret. Finally, in serious situations, you might ask third parties who witnessed the incident to submit a report.

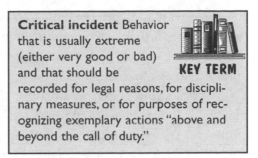

Critical incident Behavior that is usually extreme (either very good or bad) and that should be **KEY TERM** recorded for legal reasons, for disciplinary measures, or for purposes of recognizing exemplary actions "above and beyond the call of duty."

Critical incident reports are vital if serious actions are necessary (dismissal or legal action). They also show that you're exercising due diligence by addressing serious problems as they occur or as they come to your attention. This is particularly important in areas such as workplace harassment.

A POSITIVE CRITICAL INCIDENT

A man enters a convenience store and tells the clerk to hand over the money in the till. Rather than give in, the employee tackles the would-be thief (it's a dangerous but instinctive reaction). If you're the store manager, you'd want to document this action in a critical incident report. Why? First, your head office will want one. It helps management improve store safety. Second, you might want to commend this employee—even though you want to discourage taking such a risk.

Where Does Performance-Related Documentation Go?

What should you do with all these documents? Employees want to make sure there's a permanent record of the positive stuff—commendations, successes, or customer compliments. However, they aren't so comfortable having every little mistake they make recorded and sent to sit forever in their personnel files in the human resources department. Managers have to make some tough decisions.

Let's say you have information that shows an employee's production has dropped off. It's worth discussing with the employee. You want to stop the trend if you can. If you document the information and results of your meeting with the employee, do you send it along to the permanent file? Some managers do and some don't.

Those who do suggest that the information may be important down the road if performance problems recur, particularly if the employee ends up working in another part of the organization. There's some logic to that approach to documentation.

Managers who prefer not to enter "transient" information into permanent files feel they should first try to solve the problem with the employee. That way employees get some time to correct the problem (with help from the manager) before it's considered serious enough to keep as a permanent record. Managers will broach the subject like this: "Fred, we've identified a problem here, so let's see if we can solve it over the next three months. If your production doesn't come up to the standard you and I agreed on in our last planning meeting, then we'll have to make note of it in your record. If we get it solved, there's no reason to keep a record of it, since it's no longer a problem."

This approach seems fairer and more tolerant. Decisions about what you put in the permanent record depend on the seriousness of the issue, company policy on personnel files, your personal comfort level, and what seems most likely to develop good, long-term relationships with your staff.

Hints and Tips

So much of what you do with data gathering, observing, and documenting depends on your specific situation and company policy. Let's end this chapter with some hints and tips, but keep in mind there's no universal right way.

Data gathering can't be your responsibility alone. You have to trust your staff to help. For example, you see telephones ringing 10 or 20 times before being answered. What does that tell you? Only that there *may* be a problem. The only way to assess the seriousness of the problem is to find out how often it occurs and how long callers must wait for an answer. You can't stand there for hours every day counting the rings, can you?

If you enlist the help of staff in gathering that data, you've done two things. You've found a practical means of examining the problem—and you've involved employees in the problem-solving process, so they don't feel as if it's just you checking up on them.

Gather data for a purpose. Don't fall prey to "data fever," collecting data without knowing why or how it will be used. Some companies go so far as to have regular surveys and have employees track everything, then do nothing with the data they collect. That can get expensive and wasteful. Always determine why you need information and how it will be used before you collect it.

Summarize your data simply and appropriately. That's often a challenge for managers. Unless you're skilled in using the tools of quality improvement, total quality management, or other statistically based approaches, keep it simple. Tally sheets are great for counting things. Certain kinds of graphs are useful for summarizing data and seeing patterns in the data.

Distinguish between what you *observe* and what you *infer*. This distinction is important. For example, you might see an employee banging a fist on the desk. That's an *observation*. If you say, "He was furious and out of control," that's an *inference*. You're using your observation to speculate about his emotional state. You may be really good at making inferences— but unless you're 100 percent accurate, you'll never know when you're right or when you're wrong. Remember the distinction and document only what you *observe*.

This is particularly important if the documentation is used in a legal proceeding. If you write, "He was furious and out of control," an attorney or judge will ask how you knew that. A smart employee will ask that. If you can't provide sufficient evidence for your "knowledge," it's an interpretation and that's a real problem. Stick to the facts. Even "She arrived drunk" is an inference. The facts might be "She slurred her words, smelled of alcohol, and bumped into several pieces of furniture."

Some medical conditions can mimic the symptoms of drunkenness. Imagine the legal problems if you make a wrong inference, fire an employee, or otherwise damage his or her career because you drew a false conclusion. Imagine how you would feel if you made this kind of error.

Use sampling to reduce the amount of data or information you need to collect. Do you really need to count the number of rings for each and every incoming phone call? No. Take a representative sample. You could look at only 5 percent of the phone calls to get an approximation. The key, though, is to make it *representative*.

Let's say you need information to evaluate whether the receptionist is

SIMPLE OR COMPLEX?

Keep data gathering and summarizing as simple as possible so everyone can take part.

Some companies provide advanced training in data gathering methods and summary techniques, like graphing and simple statistics. That can be beneficial, but it's not necessary.

What you collect and how you summarize it should be no more complex than needed to suit your specific business purpose.

meeting a mutually agreed-on standard, and to identify ways to reduce response time. You decide to count rings before the phone is answered. Do you use one phone call a day for a week as your sample? No, that's not enough. Do you count the first 30 calls of the day for a week? No good. The call volume could be particularly high early in the morning, so response time would not be *representative*. So you might count rings for every tenth call every day for a different week each month. That would probably be representative. If calls increase seasonally, your data gathering should reflect that circumstance, if appropriate to your purposes for the data.

Manager's Checklist for Chapter 7

☑ Data gathering, observing, and documenting allow you to base performance management and improvement on facts not feelings.

☑ Documentation ensures that important information doesn't get lost. It's also important for legal reasons. Disciplinary action without proper documentation can be costly.

☑ The methods you use to collect data and what you collect will depend on your context and your purposes. Gathering data without understanding why you are doing so and how you will use it can be worse than collecting nothing.

☑ It's impossible for a manager to be responsible for all information gathering, and it's foolish to try. Every staff member can collect data and observe, so everyone can help solve problems and contribute to continuous improvement.

Three Approaches to Evaluating Performance

I f there were one perfect method of evaluating performance, life would be easier. There isn't. Nobody has invented a perfect way, although people keep trying. Sometimes it seems as if newer, more complicated approaches to performance appraisal are worse than the more basic ones! Regardless, each approach has advantages and disadvantages, so the key is to recognize the limitations of the system you're using and work around them when possible.

In this chapter we examine three of the more common approaches to performance appraisal, assess the merits of each, and provide tips on making them work. This chapter helps you decide which approach or combination of approaches makes the most sense for your workplace.

Before we look at ratings, rankings, and objective-based systems, let's define performance appraisal. *Performance appraisal* is the process by which an individual's work performance is assessed and evaluated. It answers the basic question, How well has the employee performed during the period of time in question? Combine planning, communicating, diagnosing prob-

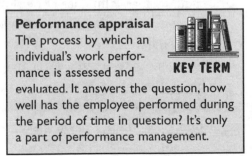

Performance appraisal
The process by which an individual's work performance is assessed and evaluated. It answers the question, how well has the employee performed during the period of time in question? It's only a part of performance management.

KEY TERM

lems, and identifying barriers to performance and you have a performance management system.

The Dilemma of Individual Performance Appraisal

Most of us live in an individualistic culture. We value, respect, admire, and reward individuals who accomplish great things. When people succeed, we give them credit. When people do badly, we tend to blame them. In an individualistic culture, we place responsibility for success or failure on the individual.

Is this emphasis a good thing or a bad thing? Let's leave that question to the philosophers. We need to consider whether job performance is determined only by individual effort and skill. If so, we can evaluate individual performance and reward and/or discipline each employee. However, if job performance is determined by the individual plus other factors (people, resources, systems), then we need to consider those other factors if we want to improve. Which is it?

Let's use our own experience and good sense. Consider the following situations:

- The best opera singer in the world performs with an amateur orchestra and conductor. The opera singer does her best, but the performance is terrible. Do we blame the opera singer? Or do we praise her efforts? Or does she get a "black mark" in her file?
- The best basketball player of all time moves to the worst team in the league. Although he scores over 50 points every game, the team loses 85 percent of its games. Do we applaud the star player? Or do we recognize that the team has failed?
- An auto assembly line has to be shut down periodically because of shortages. As a result, production is lower than expected. How do we evaluate the workers?
- A manager of a retail store is told to increase store sales by 20 percent or be terminated. At the same time his staff budget is cut, resulting in a sloppy store, long lines at the cash register, and customer dissatisfaction. Sales drop. Does it make sense to fire the manager? More important, would hiring a new manager improve store sales?

Do you see the problem? The opera singer, the basketball player, the assembly line workers, the retail store manager: no matter how good or even great their individual efforts may be, there's a performance problem. Focus only on the individual, and you won't solve these problems or you'll miss them entirely or you won't determine the real causes.

None of us is an island. Our performances are determined by some individual factors, like skill and effort, but also by factors beyond our direct control—decisions made by others, resources allotted to us, the system in which we work, and so on. If we evaluated the retail store manager above, for example, and attributed the failure to him then hired a replacement, she'd fail. The same for the next manager and the next manager. Not only is that unfair, it's stupid. The company would be firing people who are probably good managers. Most important, by attributing the poor sales to the managers, the company will never identify the real reason why the store is going down the tubes.

So here's the dilemma. Our culture and our companies require that we evaluate employee performance on an individual basis. If we focus on individual performance and don't look at context, the conditions that limit performance, then our efforts will fail. We won't improve because we won't see real causes. We'll

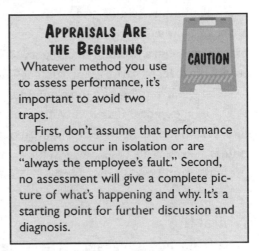

APPRAISALS ARE THE BEGINNING

CAUTION

Whatever method you use to assess performance, it's important to avoid two traps.

First, don't assume that performance problems occur in isolation or are "always the employee's fault." Second, no assessment will give a complete picture of what's happening and why. It's a starting point for further discussion and diagnosis.

punish people for things beyond their control. We'll reward the wrong people for the wrong reasons.

What's the solution? It's in the mindset. Although you may have to evaluate each employee, remember that individual performance is not completely (or even mostly) under the control of the employee. If you see performance appraisal as a tool to improve, rather than as a final judgment, you're more likely to identify real problems and avoid blaming or rewarding people for things not under their control. Then everybody can gain.

Now let's discuss three methods of performance appraisal—rating, ranking, and objective based. Whatever their advantages and disadvantages, remember that all individual performance appraisal approaches have some of the same limitations. We must always consider context and do a proper diagnosis of why problems are occurring. In other words, don't jump to conclusions.

Rating Systems

Rating systems are common—perhaps the most popular way to assess performance. That may be because ratings require the least effort. Despite some serious flaws, they remain ubiquitous. The question we need to answer is, How much value do they add to the organization and to what extent do they help create improvement and success?

Rating systems are "workplace report cards," much like those teachers in elementary schools use for their students. They consist of two parts: a list of characteristics, areas, or behaviors to be assessed and some means to assign a number or category to the item that's supposed to represent the level of performance on each item.

The "scale part" is like the elementary school grading system (e.g., A, B, C, D, F), except it usually involves numbers or phrases instead of letters. Where letters or numbers are used, they're usually associated with points along a scale (e.g., never, seldom, most of the time, always). You're probably familiar with the approach. Table 8-1 shows some examples of job criteria and scales.

Typical Use

Most companies using rating systems do so to standardize—bring uniformity and consistency to the performance appraisal process. Typically the human resources or personnel department will provide managers with a standard form—a one-size-fits-all approach, so everyone in the company is assessed in a similar way. Once a year managers are asked (or required) to submit a completed rating form. Some companies ask that all the appraisals be done at the same time (such as at the end of the fiscal year), while others use the hiring anniversary of each employee. In most cases, managers *must* use the forms given to them.

Performance Criterion Statements	Scale			
1. Completes work on time.	Never 1	Sometimes 2	Usually 3	Always 4
2. Demonstrates skills and abilities needed to do job.	Not Consistently 1	Consistently 2		Always 3
3. Demonstrates creativity and initiative.	Never 1	Sometimes 2	Usually 3	Always 4
4. Meets or exceeds sales targets each quarter.	Room for Improvement 1	Satisfactory 2		Excellent 3

Table 8-1. Some sample items often used in rating systems

SAMPLE CRITERIA USED IN RATING STAFF

- Completes tasks on schedule
- Shows initiative and creativity
- Interacts with clients in a polite, constructive way
- Demonstrates a high level of organization
- Meets or exceeds sales targets each quarter

FOR EXAMPLE

Who does the ratings? It varies. Some managers do all the rating. Others ask employees to rate themselves and use those ratings. Others will both rate the employees and ask employees to self-rate, and then compare the assessments and arrive at some compromise. However the ratings are determined, both the manager and the employee sign the completed form, as should be the case for any appraisal method.

Companies vary in terms of the nuts-and-bolts process, but typically it's a one-size-fits-all within any one organization.

Strengths of Rating Systems

Rating systems are so popular because it's possible to complete the rating obligations quickly and with a minimum of effort. A manager can complete a typical rating form in 10 to 15 minutes and send it on, satisfying the requirements set by the human resources folks. Most employees and managers are familiar with the "report card" approach, so they don't seem to need training to use the system. It's simple and intuitive—

at least at first glance. Finally, it allows a single system to be used across jobs and departments, a standardization that appeals to human resources departments.

Weaknesses of Rating Systems

The most important weakness of rating systems comes, ironically, from their strengths. Since rating systems appear simple and easy to use, managers forget why they're doing them and just get them out of the way. Sure, rating can be quickly done, but if that's all a manager is doing, chances are more harm than benefit results. That's because the aim is *never* to complete the form, but to work with employees to improve performance. No form is going to help us do that by itself. Simple rating systems help managers forget the point.

 FOCUSING ON THE FORM
Focus on completing the form, and you're wasting your time! Use the form to stimulate discussions, diagnoses, and performance improvement, and there's huge payoff. Ratings are only a way to begin discussions in partnership with employees.

Let's ask some other questions about rating systems.

First, do they give some objective assessments of performance that manager and employee would easily agree on? Generally not. The criteria used (as in the examples in Table 8-1) are usually vague and imprecise. Will any two people agree on the meaning of "demonstrates creativity and initiative"? No. What happens?

Appraisals get bogged down in arguments between manager and employee because the criteria are vague. It becomes unpleasant, which is one reason managers and employees loathe the process. Even the scales used can be vague or unclear. What does "sometimes" mean? How about "consistently"?

Another question: do rating systems provide feedback specific enough to help employees improve their performance? Again, no, at least not by themselves. For example, assume that an employee is rated as "sometimes" (below average) on "creativity and initiative." Does that tell the employee how to improve? Take a course, or work harder, or be more aggressive or maybe less aggressive? The rating doesn't tell us how to fix the problem. Also, ratings done on a yearly basis aren't timely enough to help employees improve. Rating once a year focuses on looking in the rearview mirror, rather than solving or preventing problems.

> **CLARIFY WHAT IT MEANS**
>
> If you have to use ratings, always clarify the meaning of each item in advance. Involve staff in determining what each item means. This establishes common meaning and avoids squabbling later on.
>
> *TRICKS OF THE TRADE*

Do rating systems protect employers from legal action? Often not. While rating systems may meet the requirement that performance problems be communicated to staff, the use of vague job assessment criteria may not be defensible. For example, what about an employee who often comes to work late? Is a rating of "poor" sufficient documentation to convince a court that the disciplinary action taken is fair and based on objective, valid reasons? Unlikely. The court will probably want more specific information, such as dates or total amount of time late. We need to be careful about assuming that rating systems protect the company. In many situations, they create a false sense of security. There's even some evidence (case studies) to suggest that poorly done documentation is worse than no documentation when it comes to legal battles.

Are there other issues to consider? Yes, but rather than go through them one by one, let's use the criteria for a performance management process that works, as outlined in Chapter 3. We've summarized the key criteria and comments in Table 8-2.

In Summary

Rating systems are common, but the process is flawed if ratings are the only method used to appraise and manage performance. Ratings aren't helpful in planning performance, preventing problems, protecting the organization, or developing employee skills, because they're too vague. What can you do if your company requires you to use a rating system? How can you avoid the problems and compensate for the flaws?

Keep in mind that effective performance management is about people, relationships, and creating mutual understanding. If your company hands you a tool that isn't very good, use other tools to support and augment it. Great managers will make even a lousy system work because they

Criteria	Comments
Helps organizations coordinate work of units and helps align individual jobs with larger goals.	Not by itself. Doesn't focus on job tasks.
Helps identify barriers to success that interfere with an organization's productivity.	Often not used to identify and remove barriers, but can serve as a beginning point for problem solving.
Provides ways of documenting and communicating about performance that conform to legal requirements.	Probably not. Can give a false sense of security. Criteria often too vague to stand up to legal challenge.
Provides valid information to use for decisions about promotions, employee development, and training.	Not by itself. Ratings alone give little concrete information, but may be used as a basis for generating more valid information.
Provides a cooperative forum to identify problem areas, diagnose problems, and eliminate barriers to individual success.	Tends to create arguments because it's vague. Needs to be augmented by detailed discussion to serve these purposes.
Helps manager coordinate the work of all people reporting to him or her.	No. Focuses mostly on appraisal rather than planning or coordination.
Provides regular, ongoing feedback that improves employee motivation.	Not if it's a once-a-year process.
Prevents mistakes by making expectations clear and establishing shared understanding and authority levels.	No. Focuses on looking backward, not forward. Needs to be augmented to serve this purpose.
Is simple to do and practical.	The system is so easy that it encourages superficiality.
Involves minimal paperwork and bureaucracy.	Depends on how it's implemented.
Serves the needs of managers, employees, and the organization.	Generally not. Employees, in particular, dislike the process and find it a waste of time.
Time needed to do it is practical.	Ratings can be done very quickly. The faster they are done, the more useless they are.

Table 8-2. Summary evaluation of a rating system

expand on it, use it as a starting point for what's important, which is the relationship and communication between manager and employee.

Tips for Making Rating Systems Work

Here are some ways you might make rating systems work to improve performance.

- Supplement the rating system with regular discussions with each employee about how work is going. Don't wait until the yearly review to discuss problems.
- Supplement the rating sheet or form with some way of making short comments about each item. If the rating is low, explain why. If it's high, explain what the person has done well.
- Always clarify the meaning of each rating item before doing the rating. Discuss your idea of its meaning and ask the employee about how he or she understands it.
- Rate together with each employee. Negotiate the ratings to reach common ground when possible. Involve staff in the discussion. Don't render judgments.
- Don't stop with the rating. Regardless of how you rate an item, a great question to ask is, What do you feel you need to improve on over the next year? Another one is, What can I or the two of us do to help you improve?
- Keep in mind that most ratings are subjective, based on opinion, and they can't measure performance exactly. Take them seriously, but not too seriously.

Ranking Systems

Ranking systems involve comparing people to each other and determining whether an employee is better than, the same as, or worse than his or her colleagues on the basis of some set of criteria (e.g., sales totals or management ability).

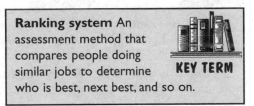

Ranking system An assessment method that compares people doing similar jobs to determine who is best, next best, and so on. **KEY TERM**

The difference between rating (using standards) and ranking (making comparisons) is significant. What if you manage an exceptionally able staff? You could *rate* all of them high, but a ranking system requires you have one "best" (however that's defined) and a "worst." Likewise, if you have a terrible staff, someone—no matter how poor the performance—is going to be ranked at the top.

The only reason we've included ranking systems in this discussion is to encourage you not to use them. They're almost never appropriate.

Why not? To explain, consider unwanted side effects. You know that almost any medication has some side effects. We use medication if the benefits outweigh the risks of undesirable side effects. On the other hand, if the benefits of a drug are outweighed by side effects, we'd avoid it.

Ranking systems have the potential to cause unwanted side effects. Because ranking systems compare colleagues, in a very real sense they push people to compete with each other. There are two ways for an employee to be ranked higher than colleagues. One is to perform better and accomplish more. That's not bad. Competition can be a good thing. The second way is for the employee to make sure that his or her colleagues (competitors) perform worse and accomplish less, or work so selfishly that the employee interferes with the overall achievement of the work unit. That's bad.

In the short run, ranking systems can encourage some people to work harder to come out on top. They can also encourage people to passively or actively interfere with the work of others. Sounds cynical? It happens—and not with selfish, nasty, unethical employees. It happens when

---

RANK RANKINGS

FOR EXAMPLE Selling houses is a tough business. There's big money in commissions, but the competition is stiff.

ABC Realty decided to award a bonus to the salesperson who sold the most property. Every quarter, the boss released the individual sales figures, ranked the reps, and rewarded the top dog. What happened?

The reps started doing only the things that would help them come out on top. They didn't do their paperwork. Phone messages were misrouted—or got lost. Reps competed for each new client, skulking around the phones to pounce on calls. They stopped cooperating. Morale dropped. Arguments became more common and much more intense.

Over the short term, some of the reps sold more. Over the long term, however, the company as a whole was less successful.

employees focus on a single goal and don't pay attention to other important goals. Rankings encourage that. That's not in the interests of the organization, since we want everyone to do well. We don't want to reward people because other people are doing poorly.

In Summary

Ranking systems, particularly those tied to monetary rewards, provide incentives for employees to want their colleagues to perform less well. They also suffer from many of the flaws of rating systems. The criteria are often vague. Rankings can be based on objective measures such as measurable sales figures, but often end up as subjective anyway. Table 8-3 summarizes some of the issues in using ranking systems.

Appraisal by Objectives and Standards

By now you've probably realized that we believe the best way to evaluate or appraise performance is by looking at the degree to which the employee has achieved the mutually set goals, objectives, or standards. Set goals during performance planning. Communicate in an ongoing way about progress toward achieving those targets, identifying barriers, and removing them. Then, use the level of goal achievement to assess performance and guide the appraisal process. Is this perfect? No. No perfect system exists.

While rating systems assess a person's performance according to vague criteria, and ranking systems compare a person's performance against the performance of others, objective-based appraisal compares performance to a set of standards or targets negotiated individually. As we pointed out in Chapter 5, objectives and standards set during performance planning are written to be measurable in some objective way. They are set individually to allow flexibility to reflect an employee's strengths and weaknesses.

Typical Use

During performance planning the manager meets with each employee to set agreed-on objectives, targets, and standards. During appraisal meetings, manager and employee examine each of the targets or standards to determine whether the employee successfully achieved them. If

Criteria	Comments
Helps organizations coordinate work of units and helps align individual jobs with larger goals.	Not by itself. Doesn't focus on job tasks.
Helps identify barriers to success that interfere with an organization's productivity.	No. Its focus on comparing employees may result in missing barriers that exist for every employee.
Provides ways of documenting and communicating about performance that conform to legal requirements.	Only in the rare situation where ranking is based on a single, measurable criterion.
Provides valid information to use for decisions about promotions, employee development, and training.	Maybe. But only when ranking is based on a single, measurable criterion. Rankings based on "fuzzy" criteria are too subjective.
Provides timely information to managers so they can prevent problems.	No, certainly not if it's only a once-a-year process and ignored the rest of the time. Focus is not on *improving*, just on *comparing*.
Provides a cooperative forum to identify problem areas, diagnose problems, and eliminate barriers to individual success.	Tends to create arguments because it's vague. Pushes staff to compete with each other, which may not be good for the company.
Helps manager coordinate the work of all people reporting to him or her.	No. Focuses mostly on *appraisal* rather than planning or coordination.
Provides regular, ongoing feedback that improves employee motivation.	Not if it's a once-a-year process.
Prevents mistakes by making expectations clear and establishing shared understanding and authority levels.	No. Focuses on looking backward, not forward. Needs to be augmented to serve this purpose.
Is simple to do and practical.	The system is so easy that it encourages superficiality.
Involves minimal paperwork and bureaucracy.	Depends on how it's implemented.
Serves the needs of managers, employees, and the organization.	Generally not. Many employees are not comfortable being compared rather than evaluated individually.
Time needed to do it is practical.	Rankings can be done very quickly. The faster they are done, the more useless they are.

Table 8-3. Summary evaluation of a ranking system

the targets and standards are clear and well understood, then the process goes fairly smoothly. An important point: In an objective-based system the appraisal meeting isn't only for appraisal. It provides the basis for the manager and employee to discuss any performance that did not meet the objectives, to diagnose problems, and to develop ideas for minimizing those problems in the future.

Advantages

Let's go through some of the advantages of an objective-based system.

- It allows easy linking of individual objectives to work unit objectives.
- It reduces the likelihood of disagreement during appraisal meetings—if standards and targets were written well in the first place.
- It's more likely to put manager and employee on the same side, unlike ranking or rating systems.
- It's probably the most legally defensible approach to appraisal.
- It has fewer unintended consequences compared to rating and ranking systems.

Disadvantages

What are the disadvantages of an objective-based system?

- It takes more time than rating or ranking systems due to the need to invest in up-front performance planning.
- It requires managers and employees to develop skills in writing objectives and standards that are meaningful and measurable.
- It may result in more paperwork than rating and ranking systems.
- Like any system, it can be misused or used in a superficial way by managers who lose track of why they are doing it.

Table 8-4 includes more things to consider about using this system.

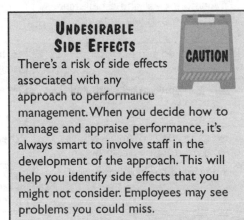

UNDESIRABLE SIDE EFFECTS

CAUTION

There's a risk of side effects associated with any approach to performance management. When you decide how to manage and appraise performance, it's always smart to involve staff in the development of the approach. This will help you identify side effects that you might not consider. Employees may see problems you could miss.

Criteria	Comments
Helps organizations coordinate work of units and helps align individual jobs with larger goals.	Yes, because it stresses planning as well as appraisal.
Helps identify barriers to success that interfere with an organization's productivity.	Yes, when integrated as part of the complete performance management system. This benefit depends on the manager's attitude.
Provides ways of documenting and communicating about performance that conform to legal requirements.	Probably the most legally defensible approach.
Provides valid information to use for decisions about promotions, employee development, and training.	Yes, provided that targets are written well, which takes skill on part of manager and employee.
Provides timely information to managers so they can prevent problems.	Yes, provided that it's integrated into the overall system and the principle of "no surprises" is respected.
Provides a cooperative forum to identify problem areas, diagnose problems, and eliminate barriers to individual success.	Depends on interpersonal abilities of manager and employee to create that forum. Since the process is a partnership from the start, cooperation for appraisal is more likely.
Helps manager coordinate the work of all people reporting to him or her.	Yes, when done properly.
Provides regular, ongoing feedback that improves employee motivation.	Not if it's a once-a-year process. But even then it makes it easier to discuss progress related to objectives throughout the year.
Prevents mistakes by making expectations clear and establishing shared understanding and authority levels.	Yes, that's the key—clarity.
Is simple to do and practical.	No, it's not simple. Yes, it can be practical.
Involves minimal paperwork and bureaucracy.	Depends on how it's implemented. Tends to result in more paperwork than other methods.
Serves the needs of managers, employees, and the organization.	When done properly.
Time needed to do it is practical.	It's practical if it's understood as an investment. More time up front saves time later.

Table 8-4. Summary evaluation of an objective-based system

In Summary

Objective-based appraisal methods require more of the manager and employee than do ratings and rankings. Both manager and employee need some skills and need to put in the time. Rating and ranking systems allow easy, superficial appraisals that may be worth little or nothing at all. Objective-based systems demand a greater investment and yield a far better return.

Manager's Checklist for Chapter 8

☑ Choosing among appraisal methods involves understanding the advantages and disadvantages of each and understanding the potential costs and potential benefits of different approaches.

☑ Any method can have undesirable side effects, particularly if it's used without proper thought and care. Be alert to potential problems with your appraisal system and encourage staff to help identify problems. In other words, evaluate the evaluation system each year.

☑ Rating and ranking systems share a common, basic problem. They often use evaluation criteria that are vague. If you're stuck with such a system, the workaround is to make sure employees understand the criteria before you use the system.

☑ Objective- or target-based systems can be made much less vague, but it takes skill on the part of manager and employee to make the targets useful for appraisal.

Chapter
9

The Performance Appraisal Meeting

t's that time of year at the ABC Corporation. Employees walk on eggshells, and managers wish they dug ditches for a living. (Ah, the simplicity!) It's performance appraisal time. Grumpy employees meet with grumpy managers. Few leave the meetings less grumpy than when they entered. Most emerge even grumpier.

Performance appraisal grumpiness is really a symptom. And it's pretty normal. Negative perceptions of reviews, though common, are also damaging. Managers avoid or delay performance appraisal meetings, or handle them superficially. Employees are wary and anxious, and perhaps less than honest. It's a self-fulfilling prophecy. If managers and employees are uncomfortable with the process, how can they work together to create positive outcomes?

Does it have to be this way? No. The reason performance appraisal meetings cause so much avoidance and anxiety is that managers and employees approach them with the wrong mindset and use the wrong process. While it may not be possible to reduce appraisal anxiety to zero, you can take huge strides in making it more valuable to your employees and, by extension, to you as manager. In this chapter we help you set up and conduct appraisal meetings so they add value and so they can be used as effective tools to improve performance.

KEY TERMS **Performance appraisal, performance review, performance evaluation** Three terms, often used interchangeably, to describe the annual meeting where manager and employee discuss employee performance, document progress (success and problems), and apply a problem-solving approach to overcome problems in the present and the future.

Let's talk first about terminology. For most people, the three terms *performance appraisal, performance evaluation,* and *performance review* mean the same thing. Generally, they refer to a meeting, usually held once a year, where manager and employee discuss employee performance, document progress (success and problems), and apply a problem-solving process to overcome problems in the present and the future.

What Makes the Process Work?

Before we talk about the specifics of the process, we share a secret with you: if you treat performance management as a complete system, not leaving out any of the parts, and if you succeed with performance planning and ongoing performance communication, we can almost guarantee success during the performance appraisal or review meetings.

There are two reasons. First, if you work with employees during the year in performance planning and communication, they'll understand more fully that the appraisal process isn't something you are going to do to them. They'll understand it as a partnership. That helps create a collaborative climate for the annual meeting. Second, and perhaps more important, there will be no surprises at the appraisal meeting. Since you talk regularly with staff throughout the year, they should know exactly where they stand before the appraisal meeting. You and your employees will already have talked about almost everything that the appraisal meeting will cover. If you're doing all the steps in performance management, the performance appraisal meeting is a review of the discussions you've had during the year.

Once employees realize that's how it works (and it may take a year or two), they can enter into the process with lower anxiety levels. That means they'll be less defensive and more open. That makes your role easier, since you can shift from the manager-as-appraiser to manager-as-assistant in employee self-evaluation.

Let's get focused. How do you make performance appraisals valuable? Performance appraisal meetings work when:

NO SURPRISES   SMART

If I had to choose two words to guide managers in the performance appraisal process, it would be "no surprises."   MANAGING
Rarely is there a need to discuss things at the appraisal meeting that haven't been discussed during the year. Once employees realize you're not going to spring surprises on them in the appraisal meeting, they start to work with you and feel more comfortable. If there are surprises, something has gone wrong.

- The manager takes on the role of helper and problem solver, rather than primary evaluator.
- The employee is actively involved in the partnership and engaged in realistic self-evaluation.
- The manager uses appropriate interpersonal skills to involve the employee.
- The employee understands what to expect, in terms of content and process, before walking in the door.
- The manager treats the meeting as important, something that should not be delayed or rescheduled.
- Both parties understand the "why" of performance appraisal—that it's not to punish, but to improve performance so everyone wins.

Let's get more specific about preparing yourself and employees for productive performance appraisal meetings. Then we discuss the actual meeting. Finally we talk about what happens after the meeting.

Preparing and Scheduling

Proper preparation and scheduling are crucial. Schedule meetings and prepare staff so they understand what to expect and that you value the process.

Scheduling

Since performance appraisal leads into the next performance planning cycle, it's ideal to schedule appraisals around the end of the fiscal year and/or around the time that the company and work units are developing their goals and objectives for the next year. You're in the best position to decide when they should be done. Some managers and companies conduct the appraisal meetings on or around the employee's hiring anniversary. The advantage is that this staggers the meetings, so managers aren't doing performance appraisals for all staff during a short period. The disadvantage is that it's harder to link individual objectives to the performance planning process for the next year.

How much time should you allocate to each meeting? That depends. If you've been communicating with your staff during the year about their performance, the review meeting is short and sweet. It's reasonable to schedule at least an hour of uninterrupted time for the main meeting. If you finish earlier, that's fine. If you go more than several hours, you're probably going to have a fatigue problem. Better to have two shorter meetings than one long one. Fatigue sets in, and people tend to become inattentive and frustrated.

SMART MANAGING

MAKING APPOINTMENTS
When making appointments with employees, try to schedule them at least two weeks in advance. This gives the employee ample time to prepare for the meeting.

Managers often bump scheduled appraisal meetings when other, "more important" things come up. Bad idea. This sends the message that you're not serious about the process, that it's not a high priority. Schedule it and stick to the schedule. Also, arrange not to be interrupted. Have your phone calls held. This is the employee's time. Make it quality time.

Preparing Employees

How can you help staff get ready for the meeting? First, they need to understand the purpose of the meeting and what's going to occur. They also need to know what they should do (if anything) to prepare.

It's hard to overcommunicate with staff on these issues. Here's a pattern you can follow. About a month before you start the appraisal process, meet with all your staff as a group. The meeting can be as short as 15 minutes. Explain that you'll be scheduling meetings with them to review performance. Explain that the reviews are part of the process to improve performance. Explain what's going to happen, and outline anything they need to do to prepare. Invite them to ask questions or express concerns they may have.

Schedule the one-on-one meetings, in person with each employee. When you schedule, again review what's going to happen and make sure the employee understands anything he or she might need to do in advance.

Finally, consider sending out to every employee a one-page informal summary memo that reiterates the process. It might be best to send it a day or two before the scheduled meeting, as a reminder of the appointment as well as of what you plan to accomplish.

Preparing Yourself

How should *you* prepare for

> **POINTS FOR FOCUSING EMPLOYEES**
>
> **TRICKS OF THE TRADE**
>
> Here are some key points to reiterate throughout the preparation process:
>
> The review process is a partnership. There will be no surprises, since the employees all know where they stand. It's a problem-solving process. You're going to ask them to evaluate themselves as much as possible. They are in the best position to figure out how they can do their jobs better. It's about looking forward, and it's not about blaming.

> **HOW CAN EMPLOYEES PREPARE?**
>
> **SMART MANAGING**
>
> Some managers ask employees to do a self-evaluation before the meeting, so manager and employee can compare it with the manager's perceptions. Employees can (and should) review their own goals for the year under review. You can suggest that they collect and bring information that might help the two of you identify, explain, and resolve any problems or issues.

the appraisal meeting? First, make sure you have all documents and information relevant to appraisal discussions. Normally, that would include the employee's performance plan for the year, plus notes or information from ongoing performance communication during the year. It could also include letters of commendation or complaint from customers or notes regarding phone calls related to the employee's job performance (again, both positive and negative).

Then, before each appraisal meeting:

- Remind yourself of your focus—to improve performance. You may want to quickly review the six points we presented earlier in the chapter outlining what makes a performance appraisal succeed.

■ Review the employee's performance planning document to refresh your memory. You might also think about how you'd evaluate him or her on each of the items—especially if you've asked employees to do self-evaluations.

The Appraisal Meeting

What you do in the appraisal meeting depends in part on whether you're using an objective- or a standards-based approach (as we've suggested) or a rating or ranking form your company insists you complete. It will also depend on whether you've asked employees do a self-evaluation in advance. Here's a brief outline of the steps, if employees have not evaluated themselves in preparation.

1. Set the climate and focus.
2. Use the performance plan or the rating form to evaluate.
3. Begin performance diagnosis.
4. Plan for the future.
5. Document the conversation.

Setting the Climate and Focus

As with the performance planning meeting, the first few minutes of the meeting should establish a comfort level for both parties and focus (once again) on what will happen and how the meeting will be conducted.

Why should you do this multiple times—at the performance planning meeting, a month before the appraisal meeting, in writing, when you set the appointment, and once again at the beginning of the appraisal meeting? While that may seem like overkill, most employees have had unpleasant experiences with performance appraisals and feel anxious about them. They also carry some other "baggage" and tend to see appraisals as a "me versus you" situation. To overcome those negative forces, you have to keep sending the message about what the meeting is for and make sure your behavior during the meeting is consistent with the goals and process you've set out. After employees have gone through the process with you a few times, you'll have less need to set the climate and focus.

Using the Performance Plan or the Rating Form to Evaluate

Reviewing performance is relatively straightforward, provided you have a clear set of objectives and standards (the performance plan) and communication has been ongoing throughout the year. Go through each objective and standard to determine the degree of success the employee has achieved toward that objective or standard.

Use questions to begin the process. For example: "Tom, let's look at objective X, which was your highest priority for the year. I'd like to know two things: one, whether you feel you've hit the target and two, how you know whether you have. What do you think?" Encourage the employee to evaluate himself or herself and to refer to information to justify the assessment. Of course, you may comment on whether you agree with the assessment. You also need to substantiate your opinion (either positive or negative) with information or observations. If there are significant differences in opinion, try to find some middle ground where you both feel comfortable. If that's impossible, both you and the employee will need to document your positions. (See Documenting the Conversation later in this chapter.) If you did your performance planning well and communicated well throughout the year, you'll find that serious disagreements about performance are unlikely.

> **TWO GOOD ICEBREAKERS**   *TRICKS OF THE TRADE*
>
> One way to get people talking is to start with how they feel about the process. For example: "Tom, usually employees feel a little nervous about these meetings. How are you feeling right now?" That gives you a chance to reassure the anxious employee. Another way is to begin by telling the employee how you feel: "I always worry that these meetings are going to be difficult. I try to remind myself that we've done all our homework, so there won't be any surprises."

What if you have to use a rating system provided by your company? Let's say you have a set of 30 items and you have to assign a rating of 1 (poor) to 5 (excellent) for each of them. How do you get the best out of a bad system?

Here's the trick. Start by *operationalizing* each item. This means coming to some agreement with the employee about what the item means before talking about the actual rating numbers.

You might say, for example, "John, the first item is 'contributes to obtaining team results.' How would we know or determine whether you've been really superb and where there's room for improvement? What does that item mean to you?" Or you could say, "John, if someone had been watching you work, how would that person determine how much you contributed to obtaining team results?"

SMART

MANAGING

WHEN YOU DISAGREE

Ratings are subjective and vague at best. Be flexible about minor differences. Arguing for half an hour about whether a person deserves a 3 or a 4 on an item is a waste of time and can poison the process and the relationship.

Obviously if you feel performance is abysmal and the employee thinks it's wonderful, you should talk about the difference. Remember, though, that ratings themselves aren't going to cause employees to improve. The real value is in the discussion that the ratings generate. (See Chapter 14 for some specific tips on handling disagreement and frustration.)

After you have some answers, explain what you think the item means and then work to obtain agreement. Once you've established a common understanding of the item, move on to the rating process. Ask the employee to rate himself or herself on the item. Then offer your assessment. If there's a difference, talk about it. Negotiate to find common ground.

Beginning Performance Diagnosis

Determining the extent to which the employee has achieved her objectives or a less-than-stellar rating is the most trivial and unimportant part of the appraisal process. The guts of the process—the part that will contribute to better performance in the future—is the diagnosis. You'll find detailed steps to help you do this in Chapter 10. For the moment, here are the key questions to discuss:

- What factors or barriers did you face that might have caused you to miss on this objective or rating item?
- What could you (and I) have done differently so that this objective or standard could have been achieved?
- Is there anything you would have done differently?

Emphasize finding causes, identifying barriers, and generating solutions. Focus on learning, not blaming. That's how you should handle performance problems.

But you should also discuss the positives. When the employee has achieved an objective and met a standard or is rated highly, determine how he or she did it. Perhaps it was by working harder or bringing in appropriate resources. It's important for staff to know what they need to continue to do to achieve success. Diagnosis isn't only diagnosing "sickness" but figuring out why "the patient is so darn healthy"!

A final point on diagnosis as part of the appraisal meeting. You can't always complete the diagnosis step in one meeting. That's OK. You can continue the process of diagnosis during follow-ups, as well as during the next round of performance planning.

> **RECOGNIZING THE POSITIVE**
>
> It's easy for managers and employees to focus only on the targets missed, rather than also on the targets hit. Strive for a balance. Be particularly alert to situations where the employee has exceeded the standards set or performed extraordinarily well. When you focus on achievements and resolving difficulties, you remove a lot of stress from the situation.
>
> *TRICKS OF THE TRADE*

Planning for the Future

Action planning is really an extension of the diagnostic process. If you've identified barriers that hurt performance during the last year, then identify actions that will keep the problems from recurring.

You and the employee need to agree on what each of you will do. Your action plans might include arranging for training or coaching, reallocating resources, and so on. Obviously what you decide to do depends on what's gone wrong and why. In some cases, the actions required may include what we normally call "disciplinary action." (See Chapter 11.)

Documenting the Conversation

Now, you've worked through the meeting process. The only remaining step is to document your discussion and the appraisal.

If you're using an objective-based system, the documentation might include the performance plan (objectives and standards), plus some means of indicating whether the employee achieved the objectives and met the standards. Add notes about the conversation as necessary. Where there is significant disagreement, note that and invite the employee to add comments explaining his or her position.

If you're using a rating form, then clearly that will constitute a major part of the documentation. However, explanatory notes should accompany all completed rating forms, documenting disagreements or very good or very poor ratings.

Since most companies keep the documentation of appraisal meetings in permanent personnel files, it's essential that both manager and employee sign the documents. The signatures don't necessarily mean that both parties agree with everything in the appraisal or the documents. The signatures are only proof that manager and employee had the discussion as documented.

Arrange Follow-Up Meetings

Sometimes it's not possible to complete the process in one meeting. Sometimes it makes sense to follow up on a few things, particularly if there are loose ends. For example, you and the employee might need additional information to determine whether he or she has achieved an objective. If so, arrange a follow-up meeting once the information is available. Or, allow a few days for both of you to consider or reconsider your positions. Sometimes, particularly where there is strong disagreement, this can be an effective technique to enable you to come to an agreement.

Once you've completed the appraisal process, it may be a good time to schedule the performance planning meeting for the new year. It's always a good idea to do the performance appraisal for last year and the performance planning for next year as close together in time as possible. That's because you can use the information from the performance appraisal to work further on preventing problems in the next year.

Manager's Checklist for Chapter 9

☑ Have you done effective performance planning and communicated throughout the year? If so, the performance appraisal meeting is simply a review of what's gone on during the past year, and there shouldn't be any surprises.

☑ Don't skimp on preparation. It is crucial that employees understand the purpose of the appraisal meetings and how they will be conducted. It's also important that you remain focused on your purpose.

☑ Any appraisal is subjective, particularly where rating scales are used. That means your assessment isn't perfect. An employee's self-assessment won't be perfect. Don't overcommit to a position, particularly if the difference between your assessment and the employee's self-assessment is minimal.

☑ It isn't the rating or the actual assessment that improves performance. What matters is the discussion between you and the employee.

Chapter
10

Performance Diagnosis and Improvement: The Key to Success

We don't manage performance for fun. We don't manage performance to get the goods on employees. We don't manage performance to cover our behinds. (Well, sometimes!) The real reason we manage performance is to improve productivity and effectiveness, however you want to define that, and to engineer success for each and every employee.

You've set goals so your employees understand what their jobs involve and how well they need to perform. You meet regularly to communicate about performance, so you have the information you need and employees have what they need. You conduct your yearly performance appraisal to identify what each employee has done well and what was done not so well.

What have you accomplished? Not much. These steps are important, but the real payoff comes from identifying why performance succeeds when it succeeds and why performance fails when it fails. Then figure out how to do more of the right stuff and less of the wrong stuff. That's the real key to ongoing success for your company, you, and your employees.

Performance diagnosis is the process we use with an employee to determine the causes of his or her success and/or difficulties. It can and should occur at any or all stages of the performance management

Performance diagnosis The process we use with an employee to uncover the real causes of his or her success and/or difficulties. Its purpose is to identify causes of problems so they can be eliminated or overcome. It's done at any time during the year in partnership with the employee.

KEY TERM

process in partnership with the employee. Its purpose is to uncover issues so they can be eliminated and/or overcome.

We need to address a fundamental issue: what causes successful performance and what causes not-so-successful performance?

Causes of Success and Less-Than-Success

There are two ways to look at what affects employee productivity. The more familiar way involves individual factors. For example, when you talk about your best performers, don't you use words like *well trained, smart, motivated, skilled, talented*? Those are all characteristics of the employee. Try it now. Describe your most productive employee. What do you think "causes" him or her to succeed?

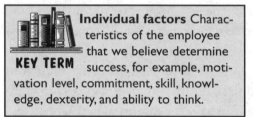

KEY TERM

Individual factors Characteristics of the employee that we believe determine success, for example, motivation level, commitment, skill, knowledge, dexterity, and ability to think.

The second way to think about causes of success and failures is less commonplace. While we still believe that each employee controls his or her own success, the work of people like W. Edwards Deming

has taught us that *individual factors* aren't the whole story. They may not even be most of the story.

We must consider the system in which people work. When we talk about this "system," we're referring to things beyond the employee's control. For example, the flow along an assembly line can be logical and effective or illogical and slow down production. Some companies set up bureaucratic processes that cripple individual initiative. Perhaps the proper tools or equipment aren't available to the employee. You can put a top-notch employee in a poor system and he or she will perform poorly. In other words, the system, the way work is done, can make it look as if employees are incompetent or unproductive, when the problems are really in the system.

Why is this distinction between individual factors and *system factors* so critical?

Most of us attribute success or failure to individual factors first. It's part of our individualistic culture to think that way. We search for the

System factors Causes of success and failure that are beyond the control of individual employees. Examples **KEY TERM** include poor work flow, excessive bureaucracy, poor communication, and inadequate tools and equipment.

employee's flaws first when job performance is subpar. The problem is, we forget that performance isn't under the complete control of each individual but depends on the individual working within a system. What's the outcome? Employee Jack underperforms. Jack's boss sends him to training or tries to "motivate" or pressure Jack. But what if Jack can't perform his job better, not because of any personal flaw, but because he doesn't have the proper tools? We've wasted time and money looking in the wrong place for the wrong causes. Plus, if we blame Jack for a problem beyond his control, we will almost certainly lose him as a potentially productive employee. Jack doesn't need motivating or training or a kick in the behind. If we expect him to pound nails, he needs a hammer, not a screwdriver. Blaming him won't help. We can help by identifying his need and providing a hammer.

You might be wondering how two employees, working in the "exact same environment" and having the same job responsibilities, can perform at such different levels without these differences being caused by individual factors? The answer is simple when you think about it. Since job performance is a result of the employee *interacting* with the environment, you can have two equally skilled employees, using the same tools and working in the same system, perform at different levels. Transfer the lower-performing person to another environment, and he might excel there. Transfer the higher-performing employee somewhere else, and he might become a mediocre performer. In both cases, performance is affected by the interaction of the work environment and the individual, and not by one or the other alone. A successful CEO in one company can fail miserably in another company. She didn't become "less skilled" all of a sudden. One company was a good fit, while the other company was not.

Another example: Sherrie, a receptionist, did her job well, answering

ERROR!

CAUTION

Probably the most common and destructive management error in performance management is to explain poor performance by first looking for flaws in the individual. Better to start with the possibility that the system is a primary cause of the problem. If it's not, then move on to individual factors.

phones and meeting and greeting visitors and customers.

After she'd been there a year or so, the organization decided to publish a newsletter. Sherrie had a knack for graphic design, so her manager gave her the opportunity to develop desktop publishing skills through training so she could eventually take on the layout task—a way to reward Sherrie by enriching her job experience. After completing her training, she was eager to apply it.

Unfortunately, the company didn't immediately buy a copy of this program for Sherrie to use. Weeks went by. Months went by. By then another staff member started producing the newsletter, but nobody talked with Sherrie. She stewed and she wondered. She felt cheated and deceived. Guess what happened to her job performance over the next year? Angry, sullen, and stressed out, she started taking more sick leave. The sad ending to the story? Eventually her performance became a liability and she was laid off.

An unfortunate but true story. The environment in which Sherrie worked (including incompetent management) created the problem. Sherrie didn't create it, but she was eventually blamed for it and punished. The whole episode cost the company tens of thousands of dollars in productivity. Was Sherrie blameless? No, probably not. But the issue here is that management should have recognized their behavior was likely to create a problem. That didn't happen. Not only did they cause the problem, but they also misdiagnosed it once it appeared on the radar.

The Performance Diagnosis/Improvement Steps

Performance diagnosis is both a problem-solving process (a logical one) and a human process (one that requires teamwork). In this section, we map out a general pattern you can use to diagnose performance deficits or problems when they occur. We'll look at the following steps:

1. Become aware of a performance gap.
2. Identify the nature of the gap and its seriousness.
3. Identify possible causes of the gap, both system-related and employee-related.
4. Develop an action plan to address the cause of the gap.
5. Implement the action plan.
6. Evaluate whether the problem has been solved.
7. Start over, if necessary.

Becoming Aware of a Performance Gap

The first step in diagnosis and improvement is to recognize that there may be a problem. How does this happen?

There is a mistaken idea that the only way performance gaps or deficits are identified is during the yearly performance appraisal meetings. That's dangerous thinking. If you have a serious problem, do you want to wait as long as a year before knowing? Of course not. Yes, performance appraisal time provides an opportunity to identify problems, but we need to know about problems much sooner. How else do problems get identified? Let's look at three ways.

First, you can identify problems through the information you collect continuously about the important functions of your business. If you're in the customer service industry, perhaps you're monitoring customer satisfaction. That data will help you identify potential problems. If you're in manufacturing, you're probably gathering information about the quantity and quality of products. However, data is valuable only if it's used. You'd be amazed at the kinds of data companies collect and never use. Provided you pay attention and *use* the data properly, you can identify problems earlier.

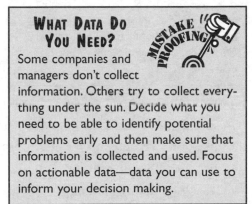

WHAT DATA DO YOU NEED?
Some companies and managers don't collect information. Others try to collect everything under the sun. Decide what you need to be able to identify potential problems early and then make sure that information is collected and used. Focus on actionable data—data you can use to inform your decision making.

Second, identify problems through your employees. You're communicating with them regularly, right? That's a key element in identifying problems: when problems occur, the employees doing the work know about them long before anyone else. Of course, they may not let you know unless they can trust you not to punish them for the problems, even when they may be implicated in the cause. They'll be more open when they trust you to focus on problem solving, not blaming.

A final way to identify problems—in addition to the performance appraisal process, systematic methods of gathering data, and communication from employees—is paying attention. Get out of your corner office and you'll be amazed what you learn. Are customers smiling? If not, maybe there's a problem. What's the atmosphere in the office? Tense? Relaxed? Try the management-by-walking-around approach. It can help you become aware of problems.

Identifying the Nature of the Gap and Its Seriousness

Once you've become aware of a possible performance gap, what's next? You need more information to to fix the problem.

First, define the problem as precisely as possible. Where does it occur? Under what conditions? How often? Is it occurring with one staff member or are several involved? And, of course, how do you know it exists? How does it manifest itself?

SMART

MANAGING

PAY ATTENTION!
Use formal ways to identify problems or performance gaps (appraisals, data gathering, and communication), but don't rely on them exclusively. Get out of your office and observe what's going on. Listen to people at coffee breaks. Often that's where difficulties get discussed first.

Second, determine the seriousness of the problem. Not all performance problems are serious enough to require intervention. The question is, How does this gap affect or interfere with our ability to achieve our unit and company goals? Does it cost money because of waste or inefficiency? Are we losing customers because of it? Perhaps it's an internal problem in a team that creates interpersonal friction. Consider two things:

- The cost of doing nothing
- The cost of intervening and the savings that will result if you close the performance gap

If you determine the problem is not serious enough or costly enough to warrant action, you may choose to monitor it in case it becomes a larger problem. If you decide the problem is serious enough to address, the next step is to look for possible causes.

Identifying Possible Causes

Look first for problems with the system—the way work is structured, jobs are arranged, what tools are available (or not)—before looking for individual causes.

Even problems that, on the surface, seem a result of flaws in an individual may be caused by the system. For example, imagine two staff members in constant conflict, hurting general morale and reducing productivity. Perhaps one or both have a bad attitude or lack good communication skills, or perhaps their jobs are ill-defined and it isn't clear who has responsibility for what. It could be that the conflict results from a lack of understanding of the jobs, because the boundaries overlap. That's a system-based cause.

Remember: don't assume that a performance gap is caused by individual factors just because it occurs with one person doing the job, and not with other people doing the same job. It's possible for person A to succeed in spite of poor tools while person B fails

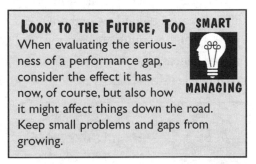

LOOK TO THE FUTURE, TOO **SMART** **MANAGING**
When evaluating the seriousness of a performance gap, consider the effect it has now, of course, but also how it might affect things down the road. Keep small problems and gaps from growing.

as a result of the same poor tools. If you identify the true or root cause reducing person B's effectiveness, you may find that both person A and person B improve.

Diagnostic Tools and Questions

It's not easy to determine the real cause of a performance gap, but the potential payoff is huge. There are a number of techniques and tools you can use, some statistical and some logical. Since our focus is on the people part of performance management, we mention a few simple approaches to use with an employee or by yourself.

THE DECEPTIVE WORD PROCESSING PROBLEM

Joanne and Mark did the same job—using a word processor to send letters to customers. The manager noticed that Mark produced about half the number of letters, with a much higher error rate, than Joanne. Instead of assuming it was a problem with Mark, the manager looked first for system causes.

It turned out the word processing software was so primitive it didn't have a proper spell checker. Joanne was a good speller; Mark wasn't, so he had to consult a dictionary, which slowed him down. Which is the better solution? Make Mark a better speller? Or find a better, more useful software package? The manager chose to upgrade the word processor—and both Joanne and Mark became more productive!

You can brainstorm to generate ideas about possible causes. *Brainstorming* is a technique involving two or more people who generate as many ideas as possible in a short time. Usually a question is presented and participants generate possible answers in a rapid-fire format. The key to brainstorming is to avoid evaluating ideas as they're presented. Just write them down. When the ideas stop, you go back and sift through the possibilities to see which ideas make sense.

A second method is called the *Five Whys* technique. Its purpose is to explore beneath the surface. You can use the technique by yourself, with an employee in private, or in a group problem-solving process.

TWO-PERSON BRAINSTORMING

John, a manager, and his employee Fred were looking at possible causes underlying a drop in Fred's output over the last four months. In dialogue, they determined the details of the problem (when it occurred, how often, and under what conditions). Then John suggested brainstorming: "Fred, let's see how many possible causes of this problem we can come up with. We'll just blurt them out, make a quick note, and not judge the ideas. Then we'll go back and see what makes sense."

Here's how it works. Define a "why" question. For example, "Why does Mark produce fewer letters and make more spelling errors?" Answer it: "Mark is less productive because he's looking up words in the dictionary." Don't stop there. Ask the next "why?" question: "Why is he looking up words in the dictionary?" You might have several possible answers for this. Pursue the one that gets you to another "why?" question. Two possible answers: "Mark is stupid" (uh-oh . . . that's not a productive path, is it?) or "The spell checker in the word processing program is poor." Next "why?" question: "Why (or in what way) is the spell checker poor?" Possible answers: "It's old" or "It uses a Swahili dictionary and we write letters only in English." Ask "why?" again: "Why is it old?"

You continue this process until you get a nonsensical answer or it's clear that continuing to ask "why?" isn't going to get you any further. Try to ask "why" at least five times.

Brainstorming and the Five Whys technique will help you improve your diagnosis of performance gaps. It's important to ask the right questions—of yourself and of the employee. Here are some to consider:

- Is the gap a result of the employee not being clear about expectations, standards, or authority levels?
- Does the employee have a good record? Is the problem a recent occurrence?
- Is the gap a result of a skill deficit, something training could address?
- Could the employee do the task if his or her life depended on it? (If no, then it's a skill deficit. If yes, it points to a psychological or attitudinal problem.)
- Is the employee capable of learning the needed skills?
- What remedial steps have been taken in the past?

The Remaining Steps

Once we believe we've identified a cause or causes, we need to develop an action plan. What will we *do*? That's a fairly straightforward process, preferably done in partnership with the employee. After you've formalized the action plan, which you may want to document on paper, you implement it. For example, if you and the employee believe the performance gap is a result of a lack of skill in a specific area, you might arrange for ongoing coaching, partnering, or training. If it's due to some psychological problem, you might make a referral to an employee assistance program or counseling program.

After putting your plan into action, determine if the gap still exists. If so, then reexamine how you implemented the solution. Or maybe you misidentified the cause. If that's the case, then go back to the beginning to diagnose the problem again.

Treat your conclusions about possible causes and possible solutions as hypotheses. Allow for the possibility that your diagnosis could be incorrect. Do your best and then, if that doesn't work, try something else.

The People Process

Whether you apply the simple problem-solving and diagnostic approaches we've discussed or you use more complex statistical techniques, success will depend on how you handle the process. Diagnosing problems requires the cooperation of those involved, and people won't cooperate with you unless you use appropriate people and focusing skills. To help you, we compiled a list of principles and tips.

- Diagnosis works best when manager and employee problem-solve together. As a manager you need the information the employee has about the problem. The employee may not see the whole picture and can benefit from your knowledge and understanding. Aim to create a nonblaming environment.
- There's a significant difference between *blaming* and *diagnosing*. Don't dwell on the past and make accusations. Diagnosis is about preventing and fixing problems. In discussions about performance gaps, make it clear that your goal is to help the employee fix or prevent the problem. Make it really clear.
- Consider timing. Diagnosing problems is least effective when the people involved are upset, angry, or frustrated. Before broaching a performance gap issue with an employee, ask yourself, "Am I able to discuss this constructively at this point? Or am I frustrated enough to mishandle it or sound like I'm blaming?"
- This approach to diagnosis can be effective in teams. If you observe that a team member is having a problem, present the issue to the group as a system issue. Focus on the overall process, and not on the person with the difficulty. Rather than asking, "How can we help Sam type better?" ask, "How can we work together to improve the process we use to get letters out so it's easier or faster?"

■ If you believe the cause of a performance gap or problem rests with the individual, it's best to start the diagnosis process in private. Never do anything in public that might embarrass an employee.

Manager's Checklist for Chapter 10

☑ Treat the performance diagnosis process as a cycle. Use the information you have to determine the cause of the problem. Work in partnership with the employee. Keep in mind that you could be wrong. If the remedial action doesn't work, start the process again.

☑ It's almost impossible to solve performance problems on your own, and management power rarely forces someone to perform better. Approach the problem in partnership with the employee. After all, if you can solve it, everyone benefits.

☑ Look first at possible system causes, and then at possible employee causes. Many problems have multiple causes: the system and the employee interact in ways that cause the problem.

☑ If the performance problem is worth addressing, it's probably also worth documenting. That means keep a written record of your communication with the employee and the steps you've taken together to solve the problem.

Performance Management and Discipline

❝ **I** 'm not looking forward to this day," John thought as he dressed for work. How to handle Brian's poor work performance during his performance review? In the last year, Brian's performance dropped below par, and even attracted negative attention from the executives upstairs. Just yesterday, the division vice president had called John in to talk about it and made it clear she expected him to do something fast. "Give him a month to shape up, John," she'd said, "and if he doesn't improve, then out he goes. You have to take some disciplinary action here."

On the way to work, John couldn't get the meeting out of his mind. John thought to himself, "I've kept quiet about this, hoping his performance would shape up. Now what a mess . . . two customers lost just this week. What the heck am I going to do? I hate this job!"

Been there? You probably understand the feeling of dread John was experiencing. Disciplining employees is one of the most trying and stressful things managers do. But it's a responsibility of management. The question is, How do we use performance management for disciplinary action so that it's likely to produce a positive outcome? You'll find answers to that question in this chapter. Before you read on, consider the following questions about John's situation.

- Given the information you have about the situation, is it likely the meeting will go well and result in a positive outcome?
- Are John and the vice president looking at discipline in a way that's likely to succeed?
- What things should have happened over the last year to prevent this situation?
- Is the vice president's "order" in the best interests of the company, John, or Brian?
- What pieces are missing?

The Meaning of Discipline

What does *discipline* mean? There are lots of dictionary definitions. If you look in a dictionary, you will find not one, not two definitions, but many. At one end of the spectrum, discipline means forcing another person to be obedient. That's a common meaning. For many people, the word conjures harsh images, images of punishment, retribution, and pain. At the other end of the spectrum, "discipline" refers to helping people through teaching and training. For example, a disciple is someone who follows the teachings of another.

Which definition is being applied in your organization? If it's a typical company, you will find that most people understand discipline as it relates to obedience, rather than teaching. Is that the best way to look at discipline? Or is it better to think of discipline as teaching?

The answer to both questions is *no*. Forcing obedience almost never works. On the other side, while discipline as teaching is a nice notion, the reality is that managers have a responsibility to act when teaching and helping fail. Sooner or later, performance problems must be resolved. Sometimes that requires unilateral action by a manager. The use of power.

We need some way to look at a definition of discipline that doesn't encourage managers to "use the whip" but addresses the real responsibility managers have for solving workplace problems. What might that definition look like?

Discipline is the process used to address performance problems; it involves the manager in identifying and communicating performance problems to employees, and in identifying, communicating, and applying consequences if the performance problems are not remedied. The first part of the definition focuses on cooperative effort in the pursuit of solutions. In its early stages, it resembles or is even identical to the process of performance management, where problems are identified and manager and employee work

> **Discipline** The process used to address performance problems; it involves the manager in identifying **KEY TERM** and communicating performance problems to employees, and in identifying, communicating, and applying consequences if the performance problems are not remedied. In its early stages, it resembles or is even identical to the process of performance management.

together to solve them. The second part refers to the "backup" approach (consequences) used when more cooperative methods fail. However, when working together doesn't solve the problem, the manager is responsible for addressing the problem with other tools, which may involve unilateral action, maybe the application of "consequences."

Consequences are whatever occurs as a direct result of an action. For example, if you choose to go out in the rain without rain gear, the consequence is that you get wet. If you touch a hot stove burner, the consequence is that you get burned.

If an employee repeatedly insults coworkers, disrupting the workplace, it's reasonable that there will be consequences. Managers have a right to impose consequences when an employee is always late and disrupting work. Managers have a right to impose consequences, even job termination, in a number of situations, after exhausting all other avenues. It's more than a right; it's a responsibility.

It's important to understand the difference between *consequences* and *punishment*. Punishment is an emotion-based reaction that involves the use of power and is something done *to* the other person. When you punish somebody, it's something you do because you have the power to do it. Often it's an emotional process carried out in anger. When you apply consequences, the other person is choosing, by his or her inappropriate or ineffective behavior, to deal with the consequences of that behavior. The mindset is different. Punishment is emotional, vengeful. It involves getting even and is parental. Applying consequences is emotion-

SMART MANAGING

MAKE SURE THEY UNDERSTAND

If a consequence is something an employee chooses through his or her actions or inaction, the employee must know in advance that a particular action or behavior will result in a specific consequence. That means it's the manager's responsibility to communicate what consequences will be associated with what employee behavior long before imposing those consequences.

ally neutral, not personal, and takes place with the recognition that the other person has chosen the consequence through their own actions. If you see discipline as punishment, it will almost always be unpleasant and destructive. If you apply consequences, it's less likely to be unpleasant and more likely to produce constructive results.

Principles of Disciplinary Action

It's your right and responsibility as a manager to apply consequences. However, there are some principles that should guide you in taking any disciplinary action.

- Disciplinary action must conform to the laws in your location and any labor agreements in place.
- Disciplinary action must be documented completely, in detail— actual performance gap, how it was identified, how it was communicated to the employee, and steps taken to resolve the problem.
- Disciplinary action should use the least level of force and pressure needed to solve the performance problem.
- The more force brought to bear, the less likely you are to achieve a constructive, long-term, win-win solution. Use strong discipline measures only when necessary and justified by the seriousness of the problem.
- The more specifically you can describe the performance problem, the more likely you can solve it with the employee—and the more likely you are protected legally if you need to use strong disciplinary action.

The Purpose of Disciplinary Action/Consequences

Think of the disciplinary process as a problem-solving tool. To use it effectively, you need to know what problem or performance deficit it's meant to address. At a "big level," the purpose of the process is to remedy a performance deficit. In the early stages of the disciplinary process, we work with the employee to identify the cause(s) of inadequate job performance and formulate a plan to help the employee improve.

In the early stages, the discipline process is still cooperative, manager and employee talking about how to improve future performance and setting up an action plan identical to the overall performance management process. Time passes and what if performance doesn't improve? When performance diagnosis, coaching, giving feedback, and other techniques don't work, discussions and actions move gradually from bilateral (both of you) to unilateral (you alone), and the focus shifts to determining what to do with an employee who performs consistently below expectations. In the later stages of the disciplinary process, the manager may be forced to act more unilaterally and less cooperatively.

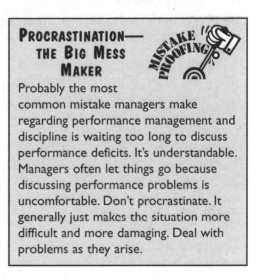

PROCRASTINATION— THE BIG MESS MAKER

Probably the most common mistake managers make regarding performance management and discipline is waiting too long to discuss performance deficits. It's understandable. Managers often let things go because discussing performance problems is uncomfortable. Don't procrastinate. It generally just makes the situation more difficult and more damaging. Deal with problems as they arise.

The Progressive Discipline Steps

Let's define *progressive discipline*. It's a process by which the manager uses the least possible pressure and force to solve a performance problem, but applies consequences if more cooperative problem solving doesn't work.

You start out gently and supportively. If the problem continues, you use a little more managerial power. At the extreme, progressive discipline can involve job termination, which is the ultimate use of managerial power. However, we always look first for cooperative solutions, since unilateral approaches cause everyone to lose something.

We can divide the progressive discipline steps into three phases. The first phase is identical to the performance management process we have described. The second involves communicating and applying mild consequences. The third involves unilateral management power.

Phase One: Identification and Cooperation

The first phase of the discipline process consists of the following steps that we've already talked about in detail:

1. Identify the performance problem.
2. Communicate about the problem.
3. Diagnose the problem.
4. Plan actions to eliminate the problem.
5. Evaluate the results of the actions.

First, you identify the performance problem. Problems can be identified through regular communication and status meetings, observation, or yearly performance appraisal reviews by comparing actual achievement and the goals and objectives agreed on during performance planning. Answer this: is there a gap between what the employee is doing and what you need the employee to do? The second question: what is that gap, specifically?

Once a problem or gap is identified, you must clearly communicate to the employee the "gap" as you see it. In some cases, you and the employee will have worked together to discover the performance gap. In other cases, such as if you observe unacceptable behavior, communicate, check for understanding, and focus on problem solving. You must communicate the problem to the employee in a cooperative and problem-solving way.

The next step is to diagnose the problem. Why is it occurring? Is it a result of an employee's lack of skill or knowledge? Is it caused by something not under the employee's control? You determine the cause to ensure it relates to the employee and to help in the next step: action planning to eliminate the problem.

Now both you and the employee know there's a performance gap and have some tentative ideas about what's causing the problem. At this point you sit down with the employee and work out some ways to eliminate the problem. For example, if the cause is not under the employee's control, then the solution might involve changing the work flow or providing better tools. If the cause is a gap in employee skills, understanding, or learning, you may coach him or her or arrange for training or additional learning.

The final step in this first phase is to evaluate the success of the action plan. Has the problem been eliminated? If so, the process ends here. If not, go back to the start of the cycle, determine if your diagnosis was incorrect, or you can move on to the second phase of the progressive discipline process.

Look for Causes in the System
As we mentioned in the last chapter, don't assume the performance is under the control of the individual employee, that he or she is incompetent or unmotivated. Check first to see if the system (how work is allocated, done, etc.) might be causing the problem or at least be a contributing factor.

Phase Two: Cooperative Consequences

If, after several cycles of identifying causes and trying solutions, the problem continues, it may be time for you to communicate what consequences will occur if performance doesn't improve. This phase consists of the following steps:

1. Identify reasonable consequences.
2. Communicate the consequences.
3. Monitor performance for improvement.
4. Apply the consequences.
5. Evaluate the results of the consequences.

At this point the ideal situation is for the manager to work with the employee to identify reasonable consequences. A reasonable consequence is something that's in proportion to the performance problem and is seen as a logical and nonpunitive consequence. By getting the employee involved in setting "fair" consequences, there's more buy-in and you'll find that you'll have greater success.

What are reasonable consequences for a chronically late employee? Make up missing time, or have paycheck docked to the missed time seem reasonable. This is called a logical consequence because it's directly related to the problem of tardiness. On the flip side, having the employee clean out the lavatories for a week is not logically related to the problem, and will be perceived as punitive and unfair. And rightly so.

After you've identified the consequences, make sure the employee understands them. If you involve the employee in setting the consequences, then he or she understands them. If you decide on the consequences unilaterally, it's critical to communicate them to the employee. In either situation, it's a good idea to document the discussion so there's evidence that you've discussed the issue. It's also useful to schedule a meeting to assess whether performance has improved. Document, then schedule a meeting to assess whether performance has improved.

Between the notification of consequences and the assessment meeting, both manager and employee should be monitoring the performance problem. If you're going to apply the consequences, you'll need evidence that the problem still exists.

At the assessment meeting, you'll review performance. If the problem has been eliminated, the process stops here. If not, then you apply the consequences.

Meet with the employee privately. Be sure you're feeling calm, in control of your emotions. Indicate that the performance problem still exists and that you need to apply the agreed-on consequences. Do so unemotionally and offer to help in any way you can.

Finally, schedule another meeting to review the problem and discuss further consequences if the problem has not been eliminated.

SMART MANAGING

IDENTIFY CONSEQUENCES WITH EMPLOYEE

It's much better if the employee identifies the consequences or at least agrees to them. This isn't always possible, of course. But it's worth a try.

Start by inviting the employee to participate in establishing fair consequences: "We need to solve this problem. I need to figure out what to do if you continue to be late. What do you think would be a fair consequence if you're late again?" If that doesn't work, state your consequence and say: "I think that's a fair way to handle this if you're late again. Do you feel that's fair?"

Phase Three: Unilateral Consequences

Our goal is to work with the employee as much as possible to solve problems. After all, if you have to use heavy-handed methods, you will likely create more problems than you solve. In any event, harsh consequences often result in lose-lose situations. What happens if the cooperative steps you've taken fail? You worked with the employee to identify problem causes, you provided coaching and training and support, and you used mild consequences to show you were serious about the issue and to encourage improvement—but the problem continued or even got worse. What then?

No more Mister Nice Guy? In a way. Management has a right and an obligation, within the constraints of any labor agreement or laws, to take more serious action to deal with the problem. If it's clear you can't work with an employee, then you may need to lay out a set of stronger consequences, particularly if the performance problem is severe. Since these consequences are strong, it's unlikely the employee will agree with them, so you'll be applying them unilaterally.

The fundamental process for identifying and applying unilateral consequences is the same as we've outlined in previous sections. You still need to identify consequences, communicate them, document your communication, monitor performance to identify whether the problem is solved, and apply consequences as needed.

Disciplinary Process in Action

Let's return to John, his employee Brian, and the vice president. We asked whether you thought the disciplinary meeting between John and Brian would be successful. The answer is, not likely. Why?

First, there hasn't been ongoing communication between John and Brian. It sounds like John has avoided dealing with the problem when it was small and is dealing with it now only because his boss is pressuring him. It's going to be difficult to work with Brian under these circumstances.

Second, at this point both John and his boss are looking at discipline as something they're going to do to Brian without having explored other options or having identified what might be causing the problem. They've let it go too long and painted themselves into a corner.

We also asked what should have been done to prevent this situation. John and Brian should have followed the entire performance management process—planning, ongoing communication, diagnosis, and formal review. If that process didn't work, then John should have used a progressive discipline approach, first trying to work with Brian. If that, too, failed, then John and Brian should have identified consequences appropriate to the problem, consequences that John should then have applied if necessary. If all the cooperative steps failed, then John should take unilateral action to solve the problem.

SMART

KEEP YOUR BOSS INFORMED

MANAGING

Because disciplinary action can create bad feelings, even if done as well as possible, it's a good idea to discuss with your boss what you're doing. There are several reasons. First, he or she should be aware of what's going on. Second, you may get some guidance and support from your boss. Third, you want to make sure that he or she is comfortable with your actions and will support your decisions.

We asked about whether the vice president's order to read the riot act to Brian was in the best interests of the company, John, or Brian. The answer is, no.

By setting and applying harsh consequences without pursuing other avenues, John and the vice president will place Brian and the company on opposite sides and set up a potential confrontation. If that happens, everyone loses. By not working with him first, John and the vice president may turn Brian into an even worse performance problem. If push comes to shove and John fires Brian, the company loses its investment in Brian and will have to select and hire a replacement—a very costly process.

Let's see how John, Brian, and his company should have handled this situation.

Getting It Right: A Worst-Case Scenario

Around the beginning of the fiscal year, John and Brian sat down to set some objectives and targets for the new year. Since part of Brian's job was to increase sales, they agreed on what both believed was a realistic sales target. Both John and Brian signed off on the performance planning document.

John set up a regular reporting system: every two months, he would sit down with each employee to gauge progress toward his or her objectives and identify problems. After meeting with Brian, it was clear there was a problem. His figures were declining. This was the "early warning system" in action. At that meeting John communicated his concern: "Brian, it's early in the year but it looks like, if things continue, you're not going to hit the targets we set together. I'd like to meet with you to see if we can identify what we can do together to turn this around. How about next Monday? When we meet, I would like your view on what's causing the drop and what can be done about it."

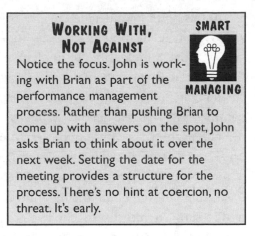

WORKING WITH, NOT AGAINST   SMART

MANAGING

Notice the focus. John is working with Brian as part of the performance management process. Rather than pushing Brian to come up with answers on the spot, John asks Brian to think about it over the next week. Setting the date for the meeting provides a structure for the process. There's no hint at coercion, no threat. It's early.

The Diagnosis Process

At the next meeting, John asked Brian a number of questions intended to identify causes of the performance problem. Brian had a list of possibilities, none of which indicated a willingness to take responsibility for the problem. (That's not atypical in performance problems.) He said, "Well, John, you know you're asking all of us to take on lots of responsibilities here and something has to give. I have lots of paperwork to do and no secretary, and it slows me down."

John was annoyed by the response; he wasn't buying it, because he knew there was more to the story. Several clients had contacted him asking to work with anyone but Brian. While the clients hadn't given reasons for their requests, John suspected that Brian might not be treating clients with respect and consideration. So he replied, "Brian, it might be that the paperwork and other job tasks are slowing you down, and we need to look at that to see what can be done. But a few clients have told me that they don't want to work with you any more. Is it possible that somehow you're turning people off?" Brian replied, "Well, anything's possible, but I doubt it."

At this point John decided to give Brian the benefit of the doubt and asked him what he thought could be done. Brian came up with some suggestions that were feasible to implement in the short term: some additional help with the paperwork and release from a low-priority project.

John agreed to these suggestions. He ended the meeting with these comments: "Brian, we need to watch this closely, because we can't get to the end of the year without you reaching your target. To make sure we understand each other, I'll arrange for the support you want, but we need to meet again in one month to see if that has solved the problem. We need to see some movement in the right direction over the next four weeks. I'll write a short memo, just for the two of us, summarizing this meeting so there isn't any misunderstanding. I'd like it if you would sign a copy to show you've read it."

During the next month, John decided to talk with some of the clients to get more details about the problem. Reluctantly, they indicated that Brian seemed slow and disorganized, often got things wrong, and wasn't helpful. One or two clients used the word *snippy* to describe his demeanor. John noted the comments.

The Follow-Up Meeting

At the follow-up meeting John and Brian revisited the issue. There was slight improvement, but it still appeared that Brian was likely to fall way below the standard agreed on. John decided he needed a firmer approach.

"Brian," he said, "it seems to me that we're not hitting the real problem here. I've talked with customers, and it sounds like you are coming across as impatient. It also sounds like you might benefit from some help with time management, since there might be ways you can structure your work so you don't feel under so much pressure. What do you think?"

Brian replied somewhat defensively—another sign of a difficult performance problem. Since Brian didn't seem willing to agree freely, John put it another way.

"Brian, I'm willing to wait one more month—if you feel confident that you can get your figures up. If things haven't changed by the end of the month, I'm going to ask you to attend a seminar on time management and another on interpersonal communication to see if that's helpful. Meanwhile, I'm going to meet with you every week to talk about some tricks and techniques that might help you."

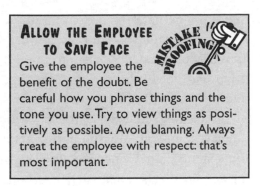

ALLOW THE EMPLOYEE TO SAVE FACE

Give the employee the benefit of the doubt. Be careful how you phrase things and the tone you use. Try to view things as positively as possible. Avoid blaming. Always treat the employee with respect: that's most important.

After the meeting, John summarized the conversation in a brief memo, which he had Brian sign. John sensed that Brian felt insulted and was resistant, even sullen. He was resisting the help offered to him. That's normal, at least at first.

During the weekly coaching meetings, Brian seemed increasingly sullen. John realized that if things didn't improve before the next monthly meeting, he would have to impose more serious consequences.

The Consequences Meeting

After reviewing the figures and finding no improvement, John took the next step. First, he applied the mild consequences that he'd mentioned in the previous meeting and informed Brian of the dates of the training sessions he was to attend. Then he went further.

"Brian," he said, "this is a serious problem. The six other staff doing jobs like yours are smack on target. We've tried a number of things to get your sales on track. I'm willing to work with you some more, but if you don't hit the targets by the end of the year, we have to look at your job classification and salary structure, since you're producing like an entry-level employee rather than a senior salesperson. Or look to see if there's some other job that might be a better fit. We'll talk about options when the time comes. But I want you to know that, one way or another, we need to find a solution. I'll do everything I can to help, but ultimately, what happens is up to you."

Again, John took some notes and put together a memo, which he asked Brian to sign.

Applying Consequences at the Annual Performance Meeting

Despite other meetings during the year, by the time a year had passed and it was time for the performance review, nothing had changed. If anything, Brian's performance and attitude had worsened. Because John had worked with Brian during the year, there were no surprises at the appraisal meeting. They went through the criteria and established that Brian had not hit his targets. The next step was to apply the consequences outlined earlier in the year.

John approached this in the following way: "Brian, I know it's been a tough year for you. We've both worked hard to get your sales figures up. I think at this point we need to discuss whether you want to consider taking another position that might be a better fit or whether you would prefer to stay in sales. You should know that, if you stay in sales, we'll have to reclassify you at a lower level. The good part is that if your sales figures go up to a senior level, we can reclassify you quickly. There are some options here, and you might want to take a few days to think about them. I can give you some additional information about other positions."

The Final Outcome

While John did everything possible to help Brian, the outcome wasn't great. After all, this isn't a fairy tale but a situation that happens in most workplaces at some time or another. Brian transferred to another position in the firm and was eventually terminated because he seemed to have developed a negative attitude and wasn't productive. Hey, you can't win 'em all.

Did the disciplinary process fail? It depends on how you look at it. The company lost its investment in Brian and, of course, Brian wasn't too pleased with the whole experience. In that sense it didn't work.

> **TRICKS OF THE TRADE**
>
> ### MAKE IT EASY ON YOURSELF
>
> If, at every step of the way, you help the employee, support the employee, and work cooperatively with the employee to solve performance problems, it makes it somewhat easier if you have to fire the person. At least you'll know you've acted with integrity and honesty. If you don't try helping first, you may have trouble looking at yourself in the mirror.

In the larger sense, though, it did work. John could sleep easy and without guilt, because he knew he'd tried everything possible to salvage the employee. Throughout the process, he acted with honesty and integrity. The company, because it went "by the book," had sufficient documentation to protect itself if Brian chose to file a legal challenge. And, just as important, the problem was eventually solved. Perhaps not in the most desirable way, but solved nonetheless. What problem? The company couldn't support poor sales performance over a period of years, but not only for the obvious financial reason. The other sales staff were aware that Brian wasn't productive and expected management to take action. If John avoided taking that action, he would have allowed the performance problem to adversely affect the entire sales staff and undermine the credibility of management.

Manager's Checklist for Chapter 11

☑ Don't procrastinate when performance problems come to your attention. The earlier you deal with them, the more likely you'll be able to do so helpfully and without anger.

☑ Always start with the helping role. If that doesn't work, apply consequences and move to more unilateral decision making. Always use the least possible force.

☑ Make sure you've done a proper diagnosis of the reasons for the performance deficit. If it's a result of factors beyond the employee's control (i.e., problems in the system), it isn't fair or useful to take action as if it were the employee's fault.

☑ Any consequences you choose should be appropriate and proportionate to the performance problem. Serious problems require serious consequences, while less serious problems require less drastic consequences.

If It's So Easy, Why Isn't "It" Getting Done? Answers to Common Objections

I f doing constructive and valuable performance appraisals, along with the other steps of performance management, is so easy, why is it that so few companies and their managers do them properly?

On one level, it's *not* easy. Managing performance requires commitment and a different mindset so you can obtain positive business results. Focus on adding value, rather than "getting things done" quickly, and it works. On another level, it *is* easy. Managing performance doesn't require complex new skills. It's just good management.

Still, managers resist because most lack the experience of working with an effective performance management system. They have objections that, on the surface, seem valid. However, a closer look indicates the objections don't hold water.

In this chapter we look at the more common objections offered up as reasons to avoid making the necessary commitments and implementing an effective, time-saving process.

I'm Too Busy and You Are Asking Me to Do More Work

The most common objection from managers is that they can't afford to spend more time on managing performance, since they are already over-

SMART MANAGING

TIME IS NOT THE ISSUE
Smart managers realize that time is not the issue. What you do with the available time *is*. By consciously thinking about the payoffs for the initial investment of time, you move from convincing yourself why you can't properly manage performance to why you must manage performance to save time and frustration down the road.

worked. Managers see performance management and appraisal as "overhead" to be avoided.

"Too busy" isn't the real problem here. Good managers make the time to manage well when they perceive value in the management activity. Nobody says, "I don't have time to take money from customers," no matter how busy they might be, because the value of money is clear. Managers use the no-time excuse to avoid performance management and appraisal because they don't see value (obvious return on the time invested) to compensate for the perceived discomfort and time investment.

But why? It's not complicated. If you do something badly and don't get the results you want and don't realize you're doing it badly, what do you conclude? That the process or tool is broken and pointless. If managers haven't experienced the benefits of managing performance, they don't have the firsthand evidence that it works. If you consistently do something badly, you tend to demean its usefulness.

When done correctly, performance management should be a zero net investment of time. The time saved from eliminating mistakes and work problems easily balances the extra time intelligent performance management requires.

If someone told you there was a new, fancy method for improving employee productivity, increasing employee engagement, preventing workplace problems, and saving managerial time through eliminating the need for micromanagement, wouldn't you be interested?

Of course you would. Those are some of the benefits of spending "extra" time to plan performance, communicate effectively, and look forward to improve performance.

The no-time excuse lacks merit. It only seems to make sense until you start to think about it. However, if you need a little more to think about so you can put aside the "no time" objection, here are a few more ideas:

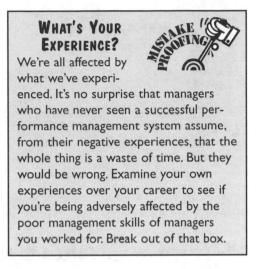

- Since the work that goes on in your department is the reason your department exists, doesn't it make sense to adopt methods that will help your team become really efficient and effective?
- If you tracked your time, you might find that much of it is spent micromanaging and putting out fires. Wouldn't you rather help employees do their jobs and not be so involved in everything?
- Don't overestimate the time needed for good performance management. Yes, it takes time, but probably not as much time as you think. Apart from the performance planning and performance appraisal meetings, most of the ongoing communication about performance, diagnosis of problems, and problem solving can be done informally. Most managers waste time doing wrong or unnecessary tasks. Reallocate that time to prevention, and you'll find time to take on new projects and improve your current processes.

What *Is* the Manager's Job?

Implicit in the no-time excuse is the idea that a manager has better things to do than manage the performance of staff. It doesn't mean there's no time, but that other things are more important. But is that really true?

What is the manager's job if not to focus employees on achieving organizational goals, helping them understand their jobs and how they contribute, preventing workplace problems, increasing productivity, improving employee engagement, and setting up a situation that adds to the bottom line?

If there are more important tasks, I'm not aware of them. Filling out

SMART MANAGING

PERFORMANCE FOR FREE
Do you want motivated, engaged employees who take initiative? Who doesn't? How do you get there? Manage performance properly, and it will happen without fancy consultants, team building games, or other band-aid fixes. The cost? Almost nothing.

reports? Meeting with the boss? What?

It's hard to argue that the manager's job is anything else but increasing productivity and the other benefits we've mentioned in this chapter. Managing performance should be the basic responsibility of all managers, not because it's supposed to be, but because it's a powerful tool to create better business results, at least when done properly.

The System We're Forced to Use Is Dreadful. It's a Wasteful Paper Chase.

Sadly, companies foist off terrible forms and methods onto both managers and employees in a quest to standardize a process that often can be neither standardized nor effective.

Are managers so helpless? No. If your company came up with a ridiculous policy—let's say that you could only talk to employees on Tuesdays—would you follow the policy knowing it would be disastrous? Probably not. You'd find a way to get around this policy to avoid disaster. Good managers do their jobs effectively despite corporate policies, while bad managers perform poorly no matter what tools they're given.

If your company has faulty tools and a faulty performance management system, you have several options. You can lobby your boss and other decision makers for leeway and try to change the system by focusing on the positive results you can obtain by using better tools. You can also add to the tool chest. For example, if you're given a ratings form that looks like a kindergarten report card, you don't need to do only the minimum (completing the form). You can obtain most of the benefits of an effective performance management system by setting clearer goals, communicating effectively throughout the year, using performance diagnostics, and so on, *and* complete the form.

It may be that the rest of the company won't follow your lead or know how you're achieving superior results, but good results will be there, mak-

ing the management job easier, streamlined, and efficient.

Here are a few more sug-
gestions to help you succeed,
even with a flawed system
forced on you:

> ### THE LEAST-EFFORT TRAP
>
> If you're given poor tools,
> move beyond them. Don't **CAUTION**
> get caught into thinking
> poor tools restrict you to
> "going through the motions" unless, that
> is, you want to look foolish in the eyes
> of your employees. Employees know
> when you're wasting their time and
> yours, so don't get caught in this trap.

- Remember that performance management isn't about the form. It's about establishing mutual understanding about what employees are expected to do and how you, as a manager, can help them do it. Keep sending that message to your team.

- If you focus on mutual understanding, you can indicate that you know the form or system isn't perfect. Life isn't perfect. Damage to credibility occurs when managers pretend they're doing something useful when everyone knows they're not. Bottom line: you can add things to meet your needs and those of your staff, right?

- Don't pretend the forms are wonderful if everyone knows they're terrible, but don't dwell on how useless the form is either. Focus on what you and your staff need to improve. Find solutions. Get employees involved in figuring out how to make it work.

My Employees Hate the Appraisal Process

Of course they hate the process because throughout each employee's career, they've been subject to managers acting as if the appraisal is a chance to blame the employee, deliver bad news, or otherwise do something unpleasant *to* the employee.

If they haven't experienced how they can benefit from a cooperative process that yields clear goals and eliminates surprises during appraisal meetings, how would they know the benefits?

When a manager decides to properly manage performance and changes how he or she does things, initially skeptical employees will slowly move toward increased comfort. When employees see that the manager is serious about helping, not blaming, they start to understand.

AUTOMATED PERFORMANCE REVIEWS?

More companies use computerized systems to plan and review performance. Be aware that automating a people-based process can result in making a poor system faster and more complex while making it appear more valuable than it is. Don't mistake the tool (whether the form or the software) for the activity.

SMART MANAGING

WHO'S YOUR CUSTOMER?

To counteract employees' negative perceptions of performance management, consider that the true customer of the performance management system is the employee. By using performance management to help each person succeed, you start to turn around their negative perceptions. Remember, you can't manage their performance without their cooperation.

Let's not be overly optimistic. It may take several years for employees to trust the manager and the performance management process. Don't expect an instant change in attitude. By being consistent, treating the process as essential, and focusing on cooperation and mutual benefits, most employees will change their perceptions. There are tons of benefits for employees when the process is done well. They need a chance to experience this and how useful a cooperative, non-blaming system can be.

Will all employees come around? No. Performance management brings a level of accountability for employees, so some individuals will bridle against that and won't see the benefits. Will those be your best or worst employees? What do you think?

If I Use a Cooperative Approach, Employees Will Take Advantage and I Will Lose Power

Underlying this objection is a set of incorrect assumptions. A cooperative approach is not a weak one, and in fact, when a manager works *with* an employee to create success, the manager becomes more influential and creates more honesty and trust. Working *with* doesn't diminish management power, anyway. Managers still have whatever formal power they've always had. However, the power of management to coerce better performance is mostly illusory. If it ever was the case that a manager could force better performance, that era is certainly over.

That said, there's a fear that if employees are active throughout the performance management process, they will try to set easy goals and appraise themselves unrealistically high. There's no question that can happen, but it's not the norm. If you ask employees whether they're below average, average, or above average as employees, about 80 percent will rate themselves as above average, clearly a mathematical impossibility.

However, when you move to specific questions about goals, whether setting them or evaluating if they've been achieved, employees tend to be tougher on themselves than you would think, particularly when they perceive the manager as fair and helpful.

In any event, the manager's opinions on performance don't

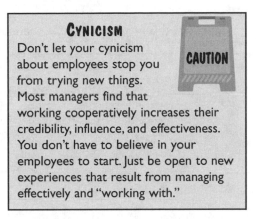

CYNICISM

Don't let your cynicism about employees stop you from trying new things. Most managers find that working cooperatively increases their credibility, influence, and effectiveness. You don't have to believe in your employees to start. Just be open to new experiences that result from managing effectively and "working with."

disappear. This isn't a move to an "anything goes" workplace. Working cooperatively means both parties contribute and work out differences. It's not weak management, and it usually works out better for everyone.

Unless I Can Use Performance Appraisal to Reward Employees (Pay for Performance), There's No Point

Managers often stop doing performance appraisals with employees when there are no rewards, bonuses, and pay raises on the table. This and the no-time objection come from the same place. If a manager doesn't see the benefits obtained from having clear goals for employees, providing ongoing feedback to address problems before they grow into crises, and all the other benefits, of course he or she will stop doing it when the obvious "reason" (apportioning rewards) is no longer in play.

Managing performance isn't about tangible rewards. It's about good management and, yes, rewarding high performers may be part of it. However, rewards are only a small part of why performance management is important to everyone.

In fact, tying appraisals to rewards is a double-edged sword. Let's take an opportunity to consider some of the challenges of linking rewards and appraisals, even when rewards are on the table.

Linking performance management to pay for performance probably seems, on the surface, to be logical and sensible. After all, if you're already reviewing and measuring performance and effectiveness, it makes sense to use that information for things like pay raises or promotions. But there are problems.

The first thing your company needs to understand is that no way of measuring the value of any individual employee will be completely accurate, objective, or valid, let alone useful. Measurements and appraisals will always be open to dispute. Tying pay increases to unreliable, fallible performance metrics ups the stakes for the appraisal process, but that tends to increase the potential for conflict between manager and employee. Appraisal plus money tends to put manager and employee on "different sides" if the employee seeks to maximize his or her pay, while the manager seeks to minimize payroll costs. It changes the dynamics and hurts the ability of manager and employee to work together to solve problems.

BE ALERT

CAUTION

Most pay for individual performance schemes have positive and negative effects. Consider:

- Pay for performance may motivate some and upset and anger others.
- It's difficult to have a system that everyone agrees is fair.
- Pay for performance tends to put manager and employee on opposite sides of the table, sometimes making it more difficult to work together.

Second, is your performance management and appraisal system precise enough, valid enough, and fair enough to use to determine pay? If you use a rating system or a ranking system or even a 360-degree feedback system, you can be almost sure it isn't going to fill the bill.

Ratings just aren't accurate enough or precise enough. They're too subjective and too easy to sway. There are many biases that make ratings inconsistent measures of productivity or employee value. A savvy employee can influence ratings to his or her advantage. Why is that a concern? How about if you reward people who are undeserving or snub people who are deserving because your ratings are subjective and faulty? What if you reward the smarmier employees at the expense of the productive ones? Imagine the anger and frustration.

More to the point, you may not be able to defend your pay decisions if there's a legal challenge. If a person accuses the company of arbitrarily denying him or her a raise, will a court accept your rating system as objective documentation that the complainant isn't deserving?

One more concern. Are you comfortable with the idea that pay for performance can create side effects that you don't want? Here's the problem.

Imagine you have a perfect way to assess how well each employee achieves his or her goals. You set standards, you measure, and reward based on individual achievement. But there's a side effect. By creating a monetary incentive to hit some specific targets, you are, by exclusion, saying that things not tied to those targets aren't important. For example, you can encourage staff to act in cutthroat ways, avoid helping colleagues, or shirk important extra responsibilities that haven't been linked to pay for performance. In other words, you can create a situation where employees forget their value comes not only from their individual successes, but also from their overall ability to contribute to the success of the team or the entire organization. You need to decide if you can live with that.

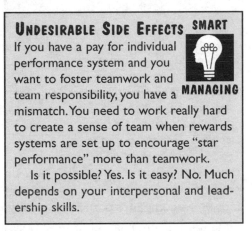

UNDESIRABLE SIDE EFFECTS SMART

If you have a pay for individual performance system and you want to foster teamwork and team responsibility, you have a MANAGING mismatch. You need to work really hard to create a sense of team when rewards systems are set up to encourage "star performance" more than teamwork.

Is it possible? Yes. Is it easy? No. Much depends on your interpersonal and leadership skills.

So, What to Do?

Acknowledge that no pay for performance system is perfect. Nor is there a perfect way to accurately assess the value of employee contributions. Is there a "best way"?

If you want to tie pay to performance, here's how to do it. Make it a part of the performance planning process. Establish the criteria for a pay increase when you set objectives and standards. At the beginning of the year, each employee should know what he or she needs to achieve to receive the pay increase or bonus. Don't tie pay to ratings or rankings. Make sure the criteria are as objective and measurable as possible to reduce arguments. And, finally, no surprises at the end of the year.

The key? Think of your managerial job as helping each employee hit that target, make the extra money, or get the promotion. Make it clear that you'll do what's necessary to help every employee succeed. That's the only way to do it. If you try to limit pay raises and play the salary guardian role, you end up in an impossible situation: the only way you can limit salary increases is if your employees fail. Is that where you want to go? In any event, if that's the role you want, you might as well give up, because eventually you'll create such bad blood between yourself and your employees that your ability to manage will be seriously damaged.

CONTROLLING SALARY COSTS

CAUTION

Managers are always under the gun to control salary costs. Keep this in mind. If you use performance management to obtain a 20 percent increase in productivity, or improve profits by 20 percent, and the successes result in rewarding staff with a 5 percent salary increase, isn't that good? OK. It's not that simple. Still it's food for thought. Don't only focus on cost control. Think of bonuses or salary increases in relation to the bottom line.

As a final remark on the subject, companies have faced the pay for performance problem for decades. Every approach has advantages and disadvantages. Before establishing company policies on the matter, read up on methods for rewarding good performance. There are other ways, like gain sharing or tying rewards to team performance or the company's performance rather than to individual performance. Sometimes a combination of reward systems works better and has fewer nasty side effects than a single way to reward performance.

Employees Won't Like Me or Get Angry if I Have to Tell Them They Need to Improve

Well, they might. Then again, they might not, and the possibility of a bad reaction shouldn't stop anyone from doing something that can benefit everyone. Let's examine the issue of negative employee reactions.

If the manager takes the position that appraisals are done *to* employees, that the ultimate decider of truth is the manager, and that the rankings, ratings, or other evaluation metrics are perfect, there will be concerns from employees about fairness, bias, accuracy of the appraisal, and a lot more. Poor performance appraisals damage employee morale, undermine trust in both managers and the organization, and have the potential to cause productivity to drop. But note we're talking about poor appraisals, executed by managers who believe their conclusions are infallible. One major reason employees get angry in these situations is that the relationship between a poor manager and the employee resembles that between a parent and child. The parent decides, and while there's good reason for a parent to make all the ultimate decisions for a child with limited experience and judgment, it doesn't work with adults. Adults resent criticism delivered in a parent-child-type relationship. What adult needs another parent?

However, when the criticism occurs within a relationship of relative equals trying to achieve the same goals, all of a sudden the earth moves differently. Shed the parent-child character of some work relationships. Build on cooperation, consideration of others' ideas, clear and common goals, and ultimately, creating a sense of being on the same side, and that "parental criticism" is perceived as constructive feedback to help the employee.

Fear of negative emotions is a poor rationale for not providing all the elements of the performance management system we've described. Even in situations where an employee reacts emotionally, if the climate is well set, that anger will quickly dissipate. Under a poor system or going through the motions system, that anger will *never* dissipate. It will fester and spread among employees.

Human Resources Won't Let Me Manage Performance Properly

As you'll see in the Chapter 14, human resources departments play an important role in performance management, but they themselves are caught between conflicting priorities. To fob off responsibility for not doing a proper job as a manager on someone to whom one does not report to is a pretty thin rationalization.

Human resources departments are not always among the most flexible units in an organization. Neither are they equipped with horns and

WHOM TO PLEASE

Your job isn't to please the HR department. It's to produce results. Or, if you want to please someone, please *your* boss. Not to say the HR department isn't important or should be ignored, but you don't answer to them. You *do* answer to your boss. Look to HR for help and advice. Look to your boss for the support and commitment you need to manage effectively.

a tail. If you feel the HR department is impeding your ability to manage, here are some suggestions:

1. Keep in mind that unless you work in the HR department, your boss is the one you have to please, and then his boss, and then that person's boss. HR isn't the direct line of authority for most managers.

2. If you feel HR is impeding your use of proper performance management techniques, ask why they insist on having things done a certain way. In other words, before you march in and state your case, understand theirs first. You may find some silly explanations that really make no sense, except to dyed-in-the-wool bureaucrats, but more likely you will come away with a good idea of what their constraints are and how you might come up with modifications that will work for you, your employees, and the HR department.

3. Once you understand HR's position, outline the problems their procedures are creating for you, your employees, and the productivity of your unit. Ask for help coming up with solutions.

4. Weigh carefully whether you should work through your boss and temporarily bypass the human resources department. Since your boss has authority over you and your unit and HR doesn't, it makes sense to a) find out what changes can be made to the procedures you've been asked to follow that would be acceptable to—even desired by your boss, and b) find out if your boss will fight the battle of change on your behalf, working at a higher level. It's often the case that a lower-level manager will have limited impact suggesting change, but a higher-level executive, talking to another higher executive, for example the VP of HR, can have more impact.

Manager's Checklist for Chapter 12

☑ Performance management and pay for performance can be linked. Be aware that linking the two changes the dynamics of performance management and the relationship between you and your employees. Keep in mind what you gain and what you may lose.

☑ Performance management (or the information exchanged as part of performance management) is a key part of employee empowerment. It enables employees to make good decisions based on sound information.

☑ Poor performance management systems abound. If you're stuck with one, focus on building relationships with staff and supplement what you "must" do with what you and your employees find useful. You can succeed in spite of a poor system.

☑ Employees tend to set high standards for themselves. However, when using vague ratings, they tend to rate themselves as above average.

☑ If you feel you're too busy to invest the time in performance management, ask yourself what your most important job responsibilities are. Examine your priorities and consider whether investing the time to prevent problems may give you more time, not less.

People Process, People Techniques

Now to the human aspects of performance management rather than the nuts and bolts of forms, systems, and procedures. Performance management depends on the ability of the manager to establish positive relationships with employees, so that employees and manager can work as partners. It's a people process that requires the manager to have strong interpersonal skills.

In my consulting work, I've talked with thousands of employees and managers in many organizations. Over 20 years I've never seen a performance management system work where the manager had poor interpersonal skills. Never! No system, no level of technical expertise in using forms or establishing objectives, can make up for poor relationships between manager and employee. On the other hand, I've seen managers succeed with no formal performance management system or a horribly designed one. How? They use effective communication skills and an ability to work with employees to put employees and manager on the same team.

It's time to look at the people process and the people techniques needed to make performance management work. In this chapter, we look at the mindset of managers who succeed at performance management. What do they believe about employees? What do they believe about their own jobs? We also look at some of the basic people techniques required to succeed, not only at performance management but at management in general.

Your People Mindset

Throughout this book we've focused on the performance management process as a people process. What you do is influenced by how you see yourself and your employees. For example, if you see yourself as an "imperial manager," someone who commands, that affects your ability to work with employees. If you think employees are lazy, that also influences your behavior. Whether accurate or not, your mindset affects your success in performance management. Let's list the essential beliefs that exemplify successful managers and successful performance managers.

The Success Mindset

Successful performance managers tend to act on the following six assumptions.

1. Performance management is a process undertaken with employees and not done to employees.
2. Except for unusual situations that require unilateral disciplinary action, the planning, communicating, and evaluating of performance occur as a partnership.
3. Most employees, once they understand what's required of them, will make every effort to meet those requirements.
4. The purpose of performance management isn't to look at the past and assign blame for mistakes but to solve performance problems as they occur and prevent them whenever possible.
5. When performance deficits occur, we need to identify the real causes of the deficit, whether they are causes in the system or causes connected with the individual employee.
6. For the most part, if the manager does his or her job in supporting employees, each employee is really the "resident expert" about the job he or she does and how to improve performance.

These six beliefs or assumptions are basic to successful performance management. Without that perspective, the process of performance management becomes confrontational and impossible. Adopt the successful mindset and you can begin to change what goes on in performance discussions and change how employees and managers perceive the process.

Essential Interpersonal Skills

If your beliefs and assumptions are the foundation for your performance management house, interpersonal techniques are the beams and supports that hold up the house. Many a well-designed performance management system has failed in the hands of unskilled managers. Many a poorly designed system can be made to succeed in the hands of a skilled manager.

To some people the term *interpersonal techniques* sounds mushy or touchy-feely. However, interpersonal skills are no different from other kinds of skills. Interpersonal skills enable you to interact with people effectively. That means building positive relationships with enough rapport to communicate openly so problems can get solved. Acquiring and applying interpersonal skills allow you to get where you want to go most efficiently.

Before we discuss these interpersonal skills with respect to performance management, we need to make one important point. The relationships you need to have with employees to make performance management work aren't created (or destroyed) only during the performance management process. They are created and re-created on a daily basis. You may be the best communicator in the land during performance management discussions, but if you act like a jerk the rest of the time, you'll harm the relationships you need. Staff will be uncomfortable, mistrustful, and wary, and that's not going to encourage them to discuss their performance with you honestly and openly. To make performance management work, managers must use effective interpersonal and communication skills all the time.

> **CONSISTENT COMMUNICATION**
>
> *TRICKS OF THE TRADE*
>
> Your relationship with employees isn't defined by what you do when discussing performance. It comes from how you interact with them every day. The more skilled, positive, and consistent your communication, the easier it will be to involve employees in performance management.

Climate-Setting Skills

By now you understand that performance management works best when manager and employee engage in the process willingly because they both understand the process and how each benefits from doing so. While they share the responsibility for making performance management work, it falls to the manager to lead the process and create a context for comfortable discussions. This is critical, whether we're talking about performance planning meetings, ongoing communication, or the appraisal meeting.

FOR EXAMPLE

THE SELF-DESTRUCTING MANAGER—A TRUE STORY

Jack was a manager who maintained a fairly good relationship with his employees. He believed in working with them, involving them in decision making, and building cooperative relationships. But, within an hour, he undid all the positives.

At a staff meeting, he "lost it" for no apparent reason. In a sudden outburst, he went from employee to employee, swearing and expressing his personal frustration with each of them. They sat in shocked silence as Jack destroyed their trust in him. What's worse, nobody dared to broach the subject with Jack for fear he'd unload on them again. After that incident, staff were no longer willing to discuss their performance openly and honestly with a manager who was so unpredictable. The outcome? Jack moved from a participatory form of management to an autocratic one. Not surprising. His employees were no longer interested in being involved.

Creating Clarity of Purpose

Focus the employee on the reasons for meeting and what the outcomes should be. That gives you the opportunity to stress the basic principles you'll be following and helps to reassure staff.

Here's a way to do it:

Mark, I know this is our third annual go-round at performance planning, but let's review why we're doing this. The major purpose is to come to an agreement about your job tasks and responsibilities so we are both on the same wavelength about what you should be doing and where you should be allocating your time. By the time we've finished, you and I will be in agreement about [topic areas]. We'll also produce a list of responsibilities on paper, which we'll both sign, and we'll use that document during the year to gauge your progress. That's how I see it going. Is there anything else you would like to accomplish through this process or anything that would make it more useful to you?

Creating Joint Responsibility

In an earlier chapter, we mentioned that one cause of performance management failure is that the manager believes that it's the responsibility of the employee alone to improve his or her performance. That fosters a climate of blame and puts the employee on the defensive. It's important, early on in any performance discussion, to make it clear that you and the employee share that responsibility and to reassure him or her that your job is to help everyone succeed.

For example:

Mark, let me tell you how I see my role. First, my job is to help you get your job done and to guide us to a mutual understanding of your job. So in our discussions we're both going to be responsible for making sure we understand each other,

> **DON'T ASSUME UNDERSTANDING**
> Many employees have had bad experiences discussing their performance with managers. That can make them anxious, even if their experiences with you have been positive. For that reason, don't assume that employees are comfortable or they remember the purpose of the process. Be prepared to establish the purpose, a sense of joint responsibility, and a helping relationship at each step in the process.

and we need to work together so you can do your job as well as possible with a minimum of hassle. My job is to clear out obstacles. On the other side, you are the expert on your job, so I'm looking to you to identify problems you've encountered and come up with solutions so you can work more effectively. Does that make sense?

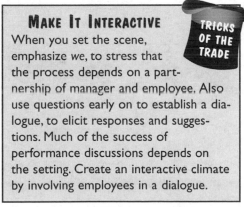

> **MAKE IT INTERACTIVE**
> When you set the scene, emphasize *we*, to stress that the process depends on a partnership of manager and employee. Also use questions early on to establish a dialogue, to elicit responses and suggestions. Much of the success of performance discussions depends on the setting. Create an interactive climate by involving employees in a dialogue.

Clarifying Process

With respect to performance discussions, employees are anxious about two things: why the discussion is taking place and how the discussion will go. We've stressed the need to clarify the purpose. You also need to clarify what's going to happen.

Here's a sample explanation:

Mark, I've explained the purpose of our meeting and where we need to end up. Here's what I see us doing. Please make suggestions about what you might find helpful. We're going to begin by looking at the goals of the company and our own unit. Next, we'll go over your job description to see if it still makes sense. Then we need to identify the five or six most important parts of your job and figure out how we can both know when you've succeeded in completing those tasks. Rather than telling you, I'm going to ask questions, because you've been doing your job for five years and know a whole lot more about it than I do.

Conflict Prevention Skills

Let's begin by clarifying what we mean by conflict prevention skills. Conflict or disagreement, by itself, need not be a big problem. Some of the best solutions come when two people disagree and then work it out together. What we need to be concerned about are conflicts or disagreements that are unnecessary or come about through the use of language and tone that cause irrelevant, sidetracking conflict. Many people talk about personality conflicts, but that's really not the right term for these unnecessary conflicts. They're really language or tone conflicts—conflicts resulting from an antagonistic manner.

Let's look at some types of conflict-provoking language and how you can substitute language that promotes cooperation and that's less likely to create bad feelings. You want to avoid provoking conflicts, not only during interactions

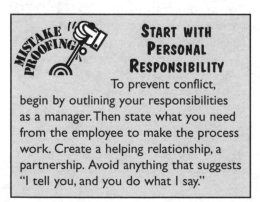

START WITH PERSONAL RESPONSIBILITY
To prevent conflict, begin by outlining your responsibilities as a manager. Then state what you need from the employee to make the process work. Create a helping relationship, a partnership. Avoid anything that suggests "I tell you, and you do what I say."

about performance, but in every interaction you have in the workplace.

Person-Centered Comments and Criticism

Comments and criticism can cause conflicts when they target a person and his or her general behavior, rather than focusing on a specific problem. For example:

INVITE INVOLVEMENT SMART

Explicitly and up front, invite the employee to make suggestions. Although you have a sense of what's going to happen during the discussion, keep the process flexible so it meets the needs of the employee as well. Even if you have a map for the process, encourage staff to modify that map when and if it doesn't make sense.

MANAGING

- You aren't listening.
- You don't know what you're talking about.
- Who are you to tell me . . . ?
- Can't you just be quiet for a minute?
- Have you even read the report?

Comments and questions like these sound like accusations rather than attempts to help. They interfere with problem solving. It doesn't matter whether they're true; they are destructive. Stick to the real issues.

Past-Centered Comments

While it's legitimate to talk about what has happened in the past, particularly when reviewing performance, it's not appropriate to use past mistakes to bludgeon employees. The only reason to look in the rearview mirror is to prevent problems from recurring—not to embarrass or humiliate.

Avoid past-centered comments that serve no purpose:

- We tried that, and it didn't work.
- For years, you've been late getting your work done.
- If I had a nickel for every time you've been late in your career, I'd be able to retire.

Guilt-Induction Attempts

Some managers believe that if they make employees feel guilty, they'll work harder. Usually such attempts backfire because the employees feel manipulated. Here are some examples of guilt induction to avoid.

- If you really cared about this team, you'd work harder.
- Most of you seem to be trying hard to make this fail.
- I guess you don't care much about this project.
- I work so hard, and you don't seem to appreciate all my work on your behalf.

Inappropriate Reassurance and Positive Thinking

Not all conflict-provoking language is critical or negative. Postive comments sound helpful—but can still cause problems. When talking about a performance problem, a manager might try to reassure the employee that he or she will be able to overcome the difficulty. Even if the manager intends to convey confidence, the reassurance might not be helpful in itself, because it doesn't explain how this is going to happen or how the manager is going to help.

Look at the following hollow attempts at reassurance:

- I know the project is late, but I'm sure somehow you will catch up.
- Things are rough now, but you'll get a handle on them.
- I know you feel like you don't know how to do this, but you'll get it.
- You'll do fine, you'll see.

Sometimes it's OK to reassure, but it's far better to reassure while pitching in and helping the employee solve the problem.

Unsolicited Advice and Commands

As a manager you have the right to provide advice and even, occasionally, to order people to do things. That doesn't mean you should rely on that right. When you provide unsolicited advice, you give the impression that you feel superior to the employee, which can embarrass him or her, particularly if you offer that advice publicly. If you're in the habit of ordering people around, it will be difficult to switch from the boss role to the partner role, which is a necessity for performance management.

Some examples to avoid:

- You must do it this way.
- Photocopy this and give me a copy.
- This is the only way to do it.
- Get this done today and leave it on my desk.

You're better off using a more cooperative tone, asking rather than telling. If you feel the need to provide advice (and it's not an emergency situation), ask first. For example: "I know of another way you can get this done that might be easier for you. Do you want to hear it?"

It Works Both Ways

We're focusing on your use of conflict-prevention techniques. But if you really want a great payoff, help your employees learn to prevent conflict, negotiate fairly, and treat people (you, customers, and colleagues) with respect. There are training courses for these skills. When you and your employees both use them, it makes performance management much easier.

Aggressive Questions

Questions are critical tools to involve employees, not only in performance management discussions, but also in other aspects of your work. Some people, however, use questions to express disdain, attack, or belittle.

For example:

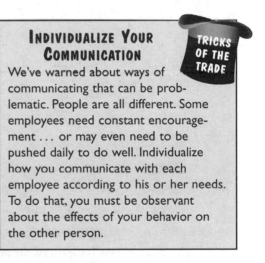

Individualize Your Communication

We've warned about ways of communicating that can be problematic. People are all different. Some employees need constant encouragement . . . or may even need to be pushed daily to do well. Individualize how you communicate with each employee according to his or her needs. To do that, you must be observant about the effects of your behavior on the other person.

- Why in the world would you say that?
- Would you be so kind as to defend your position?
- What makes you think that . . . ?
- How in the world did you come to that conclusion?

Can you see how these questions could make someone defensive, particularly if you use them with an annoyed or disdainful tone? Rephrase to sound more cooperative.

Try something like, I'm not sure I understand what you're saying. Could you explain a bit more? or, Maybe you have a really good idea here, but I'm not getting it. Could you explain why you believe that . . . ?

Statements of Mistrust

Managers, in misguided attempts to engender commitment, say things that are insulting because they convey mistrust. For example:

- Are you sure you will have this in on time?
- I've heard you say that before.

Such comments imply mistrust, which only undermines your partnership. Don't express doubt, rather work toward a position that you can more readily believe.

Imagine, for example, you're planning a project with an employee. She wants to commit to a time schedule that's unrealistic. Don't ask doubtfully, "Are you sure you'll have this in on time?" Seek a compromise: "I think it's important that we plan enough time to get this done so we can be sure you're not rushed or pressured. Can we consider changing that timeline to give you some breathing room? Then, if you beat the deadline, that's great."

Overstatements

Avoid exaggerating with such words as *always, never,* and *every time.* Overstatements usually result in arguments because most overstatements are inaccurate. When you exaggerate your point, it rarely strengthens it, because you're stretching it beyond the truth. Also, employees feel they have to defend themselves against what they perceive as an unfair attack. Some examples:

- You never get your work in on time.
- Every time I've asked you to do X, you mess it up.
- You always try to avoid accepting advice from me.

Use more precise statements that are oriented toward solutions. For example: "John, we've had three situations where your projects have come in late. I'd like to work with you to identify where the barriers lie, and what we can do about them. Let's talk first about the Aardvark project."

Notice the difference. The overstatements are accusatory—and probably untrue. It's far more effective to define the problem precisely and to focus on solving it as partners.

Defusing Skills: When Things Get Heated

I'd love to tell you that you'll never have disagreements with employees during the performance management process. That would be untrue.

Even if you establish positive relationships with your employees and work to prevent conflict, sooner or later disagreements will happen. But performance management disagreements need not poison your relationship with employees with whom you disagree. It all depends on how you handle and resolve the conflict. In fact, out of performance-related disagreements can emerge some brilliant solutions to performance problems.

Here are some suggestions for cooling heated discussions:

- When conflicts occur, focus on two goals. First, come to some agreement on the issue. It's not a question of who will win, but of finding a mutually acceptable position. Second, whatever the subject, manage the discussion so it's less likely to hurt your relationship and cause future performance problems. Both goals are important.

- Allow some room for the employee to express frustration and anger without firing back. Sometimes people say things that they don't mean when they're frustrated.

- Remember that conflict occurs when people care about what they do. Think of conflict about performance as a conversation between two people who care a lot about the job. That helps you keep a positive attitude.

- You have two options for handling conflict. You can attempt to win the battle by persuading, exerting pressure, or using power for leverage. Or, you can first understand the employee's position and then work toward a solution. The first option is more likely to polarize the situation and cause further problems. Instead, work to understand the employee first and then find a solution. That's the battle that matters—and both of you can win.

- One of the most powerful techniques for dealing with disagreements is active listening. Active listening involves paraphrasing what the other person has said so you show that you've understood his or her point of view. That builds bridges and helps the other person slow down and start listening to you.

- A basic principle to apply when dealing with an upset or angry employee is to focus first on his or her feelings. The reason is simple. Angry people aren't good at solving problems. First, the emotional energy has to vent. One powerful technique to use is empathy. If you're dealing with someone who's upset, acknowledge the feelings being expressed, rather than trying to solve the problem. For example, "It sounds like you are upset that we disagree about whether you hit your target."

- When disagreements occur, it's easy to get distracted from the real issue, which is coming up with some solutions to solve the problem or disagreement. Stay on the issue and away from personal remarks, blaming remarks, or comments you might make in frustration or anger. Adopt a solution-oriented approach. It's not about winning or humiliating or being right. It's about finding a solution.

- There may be times during communication about performance where one or both of you will be so upset that constructive dialogue is impossible. Be alert for those times. If you feel the emotional levels are too intense, take some time out. In a meeting, this might mean taking five minutes to get some coffee or a breath of fresh air. In more intense situations, you may want to stop the discussion and come back to it when both of you are calmer. Here's a phrase to use: "I think both of us are getting too intense about this, so maybe now isn't the best time to finish this conversation. Why don't we leave it for today and come back to this tomorrow after we've both had time to think about how we might come to some agreement, OK?"

Manager's Checklist for Chapter 13

☑ To make performance management work, you need to adopt certain assumptions that foster a spirit of partnership and cooperation.

☑ Think about the ways you communicate and interact with staff, both during performance discussions and in other situations. If you think they dislike talking with you, if they're uneasy or anxious, if you get the sense they keep bad news from you, then try to identify the reasons. In the spirit of becoming a better manager, ask your staff, "Are there things that I do or say that make you feel uncomfortable talking with me?"

☑ Eliminate conflict-provoking behaviors from your communication. Employees will trust you more—although it sometimes takes a long time—and it will be easier to work together to manage performance.

☑ Be a communication role model. Your staff will take some of their cues from you. If you prevent unnecessary conflict, if you treat them positively, they're more likely to reciprocate. Don't underestimate your ability to teach and coach staff so they, too, can learn to use effective interpersonal techniques.

Human Resources and Performance Management

I n this and the next chapter, we look at some larger performance
management issues. Here we look at the awkward positioning of
most human resources departments (HR) and how their responsibilities and reporting relationships militate against positive performance
management changes. Then in Chapter 15, we consider how those in
charge can improve performance management processes across the
company.

Even if you are never involved in large-scale changes, read these
chapters because you'll learn about the challenges HR departments face
and the role they can play in improving management techniques.

A True Story

When I was first engaged as a consultant to the CEO of a large company
(about 1,000 employees) to improve its performance management system, I was excited. It's rare to get such an opportunity. The CEO, Don,
had clear ideas about how he wanted a new system of performance
management that could be applied across all job categories, from directors to janitors. His stated goal was to leave his "imprint" on the organization that would last after he had gone.

He was also clear that he wanted the initiative to be "homegrown,"
led by internal staff and not by an external consultant—generally a good

PURPOSE OF PERFORMANCE MANAGEMENT SYSTEM

CAUTION

Take heed. The *only* valid reason for reviewing performance is to improve it. If your company is motivated by other purposes, not only will it not improve performance, but it won't achieve those objectives either. Having too many purposes gets in the way of making your performance management system work better.

strategy for organizational change. He suggested an internal working committee consisting of one or two employees, several departmental directors, myself, and a member from the policy analyst group, all under the lead of the HR department. So far so good.

We did a lot of things right. We met regularly to plan strategy and tactics. We created survey instruments to get input from both employees and managers, and we developed new documents and forms. We even created some positive hopes and expectations in the organization about the new system. The project went on for over a year. It was a big undertaking, and we were intent on doing it right.

When we were close to the finish line, we were asked to present our findings to the executive board, including Don, and Don's eight vice presidents. Because Don wanted a system developed internally, the HR representative was chosen to present our recommendations, strategies, and tactics to the board. It was *the* critical step in the change process. No executive commitment, no change, a year of work was in the balance.

The HR representative, Bob, stood up in front of these powerful people and started rambling on about how good the forms were and how our suggestions would simplify the tasks of the HR department. Five minutes in, I knew we were in trouble. When you present to a group of powerful people, you can tell whether there is buy-in or not. Buy-in shows itself in the body language, facial expressions, and types of questions asked. In this case, no smiles. No body language that suggested a connection with the recommendations. The questions asked were off-point, skeptical.

I sat there with a nasty feeling in my gut. While I tried to steer the presentation in a more positive direction, I was handcuffed by the HR representative, who not only lacked decent presentation skills, but completely misread executive board members.

HR AS LEADER

Expecting the human resources department to take the lead in making performance management work almost always fails. It's not because HR people are stupid. It's because HR lacks the line authority to make it work. That, and many HR people are intent on solving *their* problems rather than making changes to improve the performance of managers and employees—which translates to a better bottom line. Nice folks, but not well placed to lead such efforts.

As we reached to the end of the presentation, Bob asked for questions and comments. I knew the project was dead when a senior VP said: "All this is well and good for employees, but I can't see myself or the directors who report to me wanting to do this, and I won't use this system with my directors. You did a great job, but it just doesn't fit *us*."

Game over.

The CEO ended the meeting by saying: "I'd like to thank all of you for your hard work." You know you're in trouble when you're thanked for effort rather than results. "You've certainly given us something to think about. I'd like to meet privately with the rest of the executives. We'll discuss your ideas and get back to you on where we should go next."

He never did get back to us except to say that other priorities had emerged, and since there were some reservations on the executive board, the initiative would be put on hold "for now." For now ended up being a long time.

The Moral of the Story

There's much to be learned from this failure. While a lot was done well, we made enough mistakes to ensure there would be zero impact on the organization. Sadly, an organizational change initiative is only as good as the mistakes allow.

We'll come back to this in our final chapter, but in this chapter, we focus on the unusual challenges HR departments face in making existing performance management systems work and developing new, better ones. This is relevant, even if you're not in HR, because it explains what HR can and can't do, and how the HR culture and lack of authority mean we get systems that don't work. At the least, you'll understand why HR departments often seem to impede managing performance.

Departments and Performance Management and Appraisal

In all but the smallest organizations, HR departments end up as the guardians of performance appraisal. They write the policies and procedures. They create the forms and compile the completed forms in files, either digital or on paper. They work on a "nag" basis, as they strive to fulfill their responsibilities for record keeping, pay scales, promotions, hiring, and retention. Managers stall on getting the appraisals done. HR staff get on managers' cases to get them done.

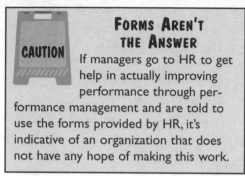

CAUTION

FORMS AREN'T THE ANSWER

If managers go to HR to get help in actually improving performance through performance management and are told to use the forms provided by HR, it's indicative of an organization that does not have any hope of making this work.

There are two problems here: lack of line authority and HR culture. Let's look at each.

CAUTION

HUMAN RESOURCES NAGGING

When the HR department's main function is to coerce, pressure, and cajole managers to get their forms in on time, you often find managers doing their best to pretend the dog ate the forms. Actually, it's not funny, and it's indicative of an organization-wide problem.

While HR departments are expected to create, manage, and implement performance appraisal systems, they lack the authority to do so properly. In a standard, hierarchically structured organization, the CEO has VPs who report to her or him, who in turn have divisional chiefs reporting to them. The line of authority cascades down until you hit the lowest supervisory levels. Power and authority come through that command structure, like it or not. But notice who's missing? The HR department. The HR department is not in the chain of command. It can neither reward managers who do performance management properly nor can it force managers to do much of anything. HR's only power comes through the line authority of the executive. HR cannot fight its own battles but must influence others to fight those battles for it.

The result is that HR departments end up in enforcement roles without the authority to enforce. So they nag or they give up on making performance management and appraisal work.

My experience in dealing with hundreds of HR employees is that the majority are dedicated, smart, and want to make a difference. It's not that the individuals in HR don't want to add value, but that they work in a system that frustrates them as much as it frustrates managers and employees. Except that managers and employees see the HR department as not doing its job. That's because HR is the visible and obvious entity to blame for rigid schedules, useless forms, and procedures that are so complex that nobody understands the point. That's not to say HR people are blameless. It's just that they don't deserve all the blame heaped on them by the rest of the organization.

HR Culture Doesn't Help

Often you have to go around HR to manage performance effectively. While HR attracts a lot of good, well-meaning, smart people, it also has its share of paper-pushers and bureaucrats who lose sight of the point of what they're doing. Worse, it takes well-intentioned people and frustrates them, and in too many cases, turns those well-meaning, smart people into paper-pushers.

When most of your job involves dealing with records, pay levels, job descriptions, hiring, benefits administration, labor relations, and so on, you tend to become more oriented to policies, procedures, and deadlines than you are to the point of all of it. HR culture is significantly affected by this, and since HR is always responsible for performance management and appraisal, the combination of lack of line authority and culture means that we often get poor performance management systems. HR is both a product of HR culture and a force that keeps the HR culture dominant.

> **GETTING AROUND HR** **SMART MANAGING**
>
> When faced with HR obstinacy and inflexibility, managers need to push harder to encourage HR to help them to do their jobs or, at a minimum, get out of the way. The best way to do that is to understand the constraints under which HR works in your organization. So seek to understand first, then advocate for flexibility.

Of course there are exceptions, but the structure of organizations and lack of authority push the really great HR people to give up or move on.

HR departments are stuck between a rock and a hard place, and the compromises that ensue ensure poor management systems. Until organizations change their structures and/or the HR culture changes, that's a reality most of us have to live with.

Back to the Story

I'm sure you can see how, in our example, the involvement of the HR department was both a necessity and a curse. It was made worse by some dubious choices. The HR representative was, by far, the weakest member of the HR department and the least flexible, most fearful, and least accomplished. If you had to choose a change leader, you couldn't have done worse. So why was he chosen and not someone more capable? I could never get a definitive answer, but I'm convinced the HR culture was at the heart of it.

The HR director found the least busy person in the department and decided to use this surplus resource for something useful. That he was so ill-equipped to do the job was beside the point. HR people like to optimize resources—it's their job to do so and it's part of the culture, the unpleasant side effect being a focus on detail and losing the point, which, in turn, created a lot of work and no results.

HR departments are busy as they try to juggle a range of tasks, so it's no surprise that the onus is on getting things done, even if business results don't happen.

All of this might have worked if Bob hadn't done the presentation to the executive board. That was another bad choice. No amount of arguing or influence, either with HR, with the CEO, or within the working group, could get this changed. Again, we had responsibility without authority, this time for me as a consultant.

Let's wrap up the story by restating some key themes that affect what HR departments can and can't do, the roles they *can* effectively take on, and what they offer to managers and employees, particularly with reference to appraisals and performance management.

While HR departments are accountable for a number of organizational processes, they often have little authority to get their work done.

Authority levels for performance management systems lie with executives and managers, so the only way HR can access this is through its ability to enlist executive champions to fight the battles for it—to get the executives to make things happen.

The culture of HR tends to militate against its ability to lead new initiatives effectively.

What Should HR's Role Be in Performance Management?

In organizations, roles must be determined by answering one question: Who is best suited to getting it done? If you answer that question objectively and focus on creating results, you can determine who should be tasked with what, based on who is most likely to create the results you want. It's not always a black-and-white thing, but where performance management responsibilities are involved, it's clear what HR can and can't do.

> **KEY TERM**
>
> **Executive champions** Those at the top of the organization hierarchy who have sufficient formal authority and a strong commitment to a particular point of view—in this context, the use of performance management as a key to improving organizational effectiveness—and the bottom line. Executive champions advocate for change both up and down the hierarchy and across divisions through their interactions with other executives at their own level.

First, what roles will HR fail at? Since HR has no line authority, it can't be effective in coercing managers to plan and evaluate performance. It can't ensure that forms are returned on time, let alone whether those forms represent a constructive discussion aimed at improving performance. Just because a company wants centralized record keeping doesn't justify dumping responsibilities on HR, knowing it will fail at those responsibilities.

Second, the culture of HR, coupled with a lack of line authority, suggests having HR play a formal leadership role in getting managers to manage performance properly doesn't work. That's not to say HR has nothing to offer in this respect. It does. But it can't take on the responsibility of getting managers to manage properly. Help, yes, but be the prominent leader for performance management? No.

What does that leave? How can HR help manage performance within the constraints that exist in most organizations?

- HR can be effective in providing a central information system where documentation of performance, forms, etc., can be stored and accessed easily from a central location. That works. But it shouldn't be the paper police officer. That doesn't work.

- As with most functions HR departments carry out, they're best suited to advise and teach. That's something HR people can do, provided they understand their own lack of authority. Both teaching and advising, whether of executives, middle managers, supervisors, and even employees, can have powerful results as part of an overall strategy to improve performance management across the enterprise.

- HR employees should be involved in helping managers solve problems—personnel problems, difficult employee problems, training problems, and so on.

- In pursuit of effective problem solving, HR should enable managers to get the things done that they feel are important to manage effectively. Not only does that mean helping, but it also means getting out of the way and/or removing barriers and hassles.

- HR should provide managers with the tools to do the job. That doesn't mean insisting on what works best for HR. It means offering a range of tools—help with planning, effective evaluation forms and tools, and guidelines (not rules) for dealing with disciplinary issues. While too many options confuse people, enabling managers to use what makes sense to them for improving performance is far better than deciding *for* managers how they should improve performance. Get rid of universal, lock-stepped performance management processes.

- In a few situations where HR is better connected to important issues, such as lawsuit prevention, EEOC complaints, or equity issues, HR is the department best suited (due to its understanding of complex issues) to advise and even pressure managers to conform to laws and practices that, if ignored, could put the company at risk.

In case it's not immediately obvious, when it comes to performance management, executives, managers, and employees are the HR customers. HR does not dictate what must be done isolated from what the organization needs to improve performance. It helps. It explains. It teaches. It provides tools.

Who *Is* Responsible for Getting Performance Management Working?

It's a bit cowardly to say, "OK, HR shouldn't be doing this" without covering who *should* be doing that which shouldn't belong to HR.

> **IF YOU ARE IN HR ...** TRICKS OF THE TRADE
>
> For HR professionals to make a difference and demonstrably contribute to the health of the organization, it's necessary to serve managers and employees, and not to focus on making HR-related tasks easier. Seek to enable rather than control things over which you have no authority.

In fact, it's an easy issue. The chain of command has both the authority and the responsibility for ensuring each manager is managing performance and creating results. Executives need to make the proper application of performance management to productivity part of the job responsibilities of their subordinates. Executives need to hold managers accountable for setting goals with employees, deciding on metrics, communicating throughout the year, diagnosing and fixing problems, and appraising performance. In turn the subordinates cascade the process down to their subordinates, and so on.

If you want better performance and productivity, top executives must commit to the processes by which these results are created. They do this by modeling the behavior they want from their subordinates and holding them accountable for doing this. Executives are the ones to make it all work. No commitment, no success.

For the Manager—The Role of HR with Respect to You

So far, our discussion of HR roles with respect to performance management is probably of most interest to HR personnel and those responsible for getting performance management to work across the enterprise. Now let's look at how managers can think about and use what HR should be offering.

Note: for every responsibility on the part of one party (in this case, HR), there is a corresponding responsibility for the second party (i.e., manager and employee). If HR is responsible for record keeping, the manager's responsibility is to do his or her best not to get in its way, in the same way the manager wants HR to stay out of the way. If HR's responsibility is to educate managers about how to properly improve productivity using performance management tools, the manager has a responsibility to

- listen
- test the advice
- to seek advice as needed

It can't work any other way, and managers need to stop dumping the responsibility for a poor performance management system in the lap of HR. When both parties do their parts to meet their responsibilities, miracles happen. So let's go through some points on where performance management, HR, and the manager intersect.

SMART MANAGING

DON'T BLAME HR

While it's true that many HR units set up roadblocks to overcome, managers who blame their own failures in managing performance on HR are not doing their jobs. No amount of blaming HR will hide poor techniques by line managers.

HR isn't responsible for solving performance issues in your unit. That's the manager's responsibility. So looking for HR to fire, transfer, discipline, or otherwise intervene in situations that are primarily between you and an employee is a cop-out. You get paid to manage. HR doesn't. HR is responsible for helping, advising, guiding, teaching, and keeping you out of legal and moral trouble with respect to performance management. Use HR. Don't assume its purpose is to complicate your life with paperwork. Don't assume the paperwork is an exercise in pointless bureaucracy. It could be there are good reasons to do it—reasons that involve protecting you, protecting the employee, protecting the company from real threats.

Managers are responsible for communicating their need for help and advice in proactive ways. It's not enough to wait for HR to nag you about performance appraisal forms. Ask for what you need. Inform HR about any challenges you face. Solicit advice. You can choose not to take it, provided you listened with an open mind.

If you have people reporting to you with managerial and supervisory responsibilities, hold them accountable for executing all the components of performance management with their staff. It's been said before in this chapter, but it deserves repeating: you can't dump this onto HR, because it lacks the authority.

Once you start doing this and you model what you want for HR, it will require less and less attention from you. Performance management becomes an "organizational habit."

In situations where HR impedes effective performance management, it's your responsibility to do something about it in a constructive, non-blaming manner. Go up *your* chain of command to elicit the help and cooperation you need. Often an executive from one division can interact with an executive in charge of HR in ways you can't. Enlist a performance management champion. Remember this: if you get fired by virtue of HR procedures that interfere with your ability to improve productivity, it will be small consolation to blame HR. Performance management is *the* key to improving productivity. And *you* will be accountable eventually, not HR, even if it's HR's fault.

Manager's Checklist for Chapter 14

☑ Human resources departments make poor leaders in the quest for better performance management because they lack line authority.

☑ Human resources professionals are often frustrated at their lack of authority. While many could be leaders in improving performance, they have many constraints and cultural issues that impede their ability to help.

☑ Advice to HR: if you can't help because of the constraints you work under, at least get out of the way of managers who really want to use performance management properly.

☑ Managers who blame HR for their own inability to manage performance in their units aren't doing their jobs. Rather than blaming, first understand the constraints under which HR operates and be clear how you want HR to help.

Revamping Performance Management Across the Enterprise

O n a regular basis CEOs and C-Suite executives indicate their dissatisfaction with the performance management systems in their companies. For example, Sibson Consulting surveyed senior-level HR people and found that less than half (47 percent) felt their performance appraisal systems helped their organization achieve their strategic goals. About 15 percent positively disagreed while the rest had no strong opinion. These findings are consistent across time and across research methodologies. CEOs and executives don't believe the systems used are useful.

Is it any wonder that companies regularly seek to revamp their systems? Of course not. Executives believe with good reason that managing performance is critical to success. Yet, they are unhappy with what they've got. So the message goes out: fix it.

Companies end up in a common cycle. The boss says, "Fix it." Those below are charged with revamping the system. There's a lot of activity, ending up with a system that, cosmetics aside, functions like the "broken one." Every time this cycle is repeated, it reinforces managers' and employees' negative perceptions of performance management. More important, it erodes their confidence in the credibility of the executives running the company. Nothing is worse for morale and employee engagement than a lot of fuss, a lot of promises that, well, end up signifying nothing.

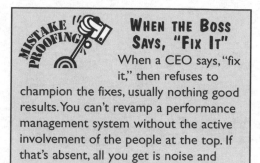

WHEN THE BOSS SAYS, "FIX IT"
When a CEO says, "fix it," then refuses to champion the fixes, usually nothing good results. You can't revamp a performance management system without the active involvement of the people at the top. If that's absent, all you get is noise and useless activity.

That's certainly what happened in the case study mentioned at the beginning of the previous chapter. What's going on, and how can we revamp existing performance management systems to create something new, something more useful and more effective?

First, the Errors

Let's consider why enterprisewide attempts to improve performance management systems fail. What mistakes are made? Not to be negative, but there's a host of possible errors companies commit.

Static Mindset = Same Old, Same Old

If you come at a problem you've tried to fix repeatedly and you bring to the task the same mindset and thinking that underlie the previous failures, you'll fail. Weight loss is a good example. People attempt to shed pounds, but often end up a year or two down the road as heavy or heavier than when they started. Did they lack commitment? Did they lack an understanding of the relationship of calories, what they put in their mouths, and burning calories? No. The problem is they bring to the table the same underlying attitudes to food and exercise, so they repeat their mistakes. Nobody suggests they should abolish eating or scrap the whole effort like some do with performance appraisal, though.

With performance management and appraisal, if you start off with the wrong mindset, attitude, and goals, it's almost impossible to make headway. If, for example, managers see performance appraisals as something they do to employees—a means of controlling them or a way to deal with the tiny percentage of poorly functioning employees, you'll get exactly what you had before. You can change the forms. Heck, change the frequency of evaluations, even. Train people to rate more effectively. Go whole hog. All you'll do is waste money and time and draw heavily from the "credibility bank" that's so important in generating employee engagement.

If decision makers, the drivers of revamping efforts, don't reconceptualize what performance management is for, it will all be for nothing.

Impatience—Wanting Everything *Now*

Nobody wants to wait five years to see the positive effects of a better performance management system, least of all executives. As a result, revamping these systems across the enterprise takes on the feel of a project rather than a fundamental change in how the organization operates. Typically, the executives form a team, maybe hire a consultant, and set a deadline for completion. Come implementation time, they lose interest and withdraw from the process—if they were ever actually involved in the first place—and, of course, when it comes to this kind of organizational change, inertia sets in and everything drifts back to where it started.

> **THE SAVING GRACE**   SMART
>
> Here's an amazing thought. A single manager can have a significant impact on how work gets done and performance **MANAGING** management in the work unit without the support of top executives and without the help of human resources— provided the executives and HR department get out of the way, just enough for the manager to use his or her skills.

The analogy with weight loss applies. Big start, loud start. Some initial progress. Then as progress slows, frustration sets in, and since nothing significant has changed (yet), there's a drift back to the starting point. Impatience and treating the revamping process as a project with a beginning date and an end date doesn't work because the project isn't ongoing and doesn't result in fundamental changes in mindset.

In both weight loss and revamping performance management systems, only a long-term outlook, accompanied by a long-term commitment and great patience, works.

Superficial Changes Always Win

Janice, the CEO of a midsize company said: "These appraisal forms are a waste of time. Managers hate them, employees hate them, nobody wants to do them, so how can they be useful? I want a proposal on my desk by end of next week with a plan to fix this."

Everyone recognizes the truth of Janice's statements, so those charged with the responsibility for revamping the system work diligently to do Janice's bidding. Skipping ahead a few years, Frederick, the new CEO—Janice has moved on—is saying the same thing.

What happened? Most times, the forms will have been "improved." Maybe they changed rating scales from a five-point scale to a seven-point scale. The color of the forms probably changed. Policy documents were rewritten. And so on.

AVOID THE EASY CHANGE
Be alert to the seductive-ness of superficial changes in forms, dates, and policies. They are the low-hanging fruit, easy to grasp, and not tasty at all. In attempts to revamp the performance management system, people will *always* drift to making superficial changes that don't improve the system or perfor-mance at all. Be alert.

The operative rule is that superficial changes are easy and often visible, so that's what gets changed. It's easy to change the color of the evalua-tion forms. Everyone using them will notice. "Hey, the new forms are green, not pink!" The people who were asked by Janice to fix things congratulate each other on their great progress, and the rest of the organization laughs cynically. Until the next time, when the forms might end up pink again.

It's not that people are stupid, so let's not portray them as such. As human beings, we all tend to "fix things" by grabbing the low-hanging fruit and by virtue of the time constraints. Want to lose weight? Eat six smaller meals a day. Rather than having your six chocolate bars at night, have them spaced out during the day. Want a better performance man-agement system? Change the forms.

Misunderstanding How Organizational Change Works

Performance management and appraisal exist in a sea of attitudes, pre-conceptions and prejudices, negative past experiences, and cynicism. If you don't understand that and you don't alter these underlying issues, you can't change anything. Revamping a performance management sys-tem across the enterprise is a special case of changing the culture and thinking of the organization, but more specifically, it's about moving every individual to a different "space," one that supports new thinking and open-mindedness about the new system. It takes time. It requires leadership from the top. You don't plant a garden and then forget about it, assuming someone else will water and weed it for you. It's your garden. You have to keep an eye on it. Occasionally, you interact with the cucumbers or

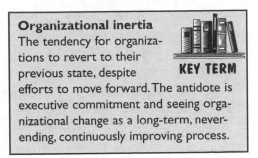

Organizational inertia
The tendency for organizations to revert to their previous state, despite efforts to move forward. The antidote is executive commitment and seeing organizational change as a long-term, never-ending, continuously improving process.

KEY TERM

tomatoes to see how they're doing and to remedy concerns or complaints.

More Errors, More Failures

Before we help you with solutions, let's list two more common errors that result in going on the revamping expedition only to end up camping in the same old backyard. The following issues are self-explanatory or at least should be at this point in the book.

- Not placing managers and employees at the head of the line when it comes to stakeholders. If managers and employees don't see the value added for any process, or at least potential value added, things won't get better.
- Not involving both managers and employees in the design and implementation of the new system. If the HR department designs the new system, it will reflect HR's notions of what managers and employees need. If the executive group designs it, it will reflect their needs, not those of the people the system is intended to help.

Leaders/executives who are too busy to lead the process of organizational change will also be too busy to achieve the benefits of a different way of managing individual, work unit, and enterprise performance.

HR departments are usually singled out to lead the development and implementation of a new performance management system. This almost always results in failure. Delegation of an enterprisewide change to a unit without the needed credibility and authority to make it work always fails, no matter how skilled the HR folks are.

Too many conflicting goals for the "new" performance management and appraisal system—for example, wanting to use it to determine pay while trying to create a more cooperative endeavor—results in a system that does nothing well.

Poor communication and training in the new system allow inertia-like cynicism to creep in and sabotage the process. If you can't change how people think about appraisals and managing performance and you don't change how people feel about those things, you can't get more than surface compliance.

Measuring the success of a new performance management system by counting how many managers complete the forms and submit them on time to the HR department is pointless and, once again, encourages surface compliance—doing forms, shuffling papers. Performance management and appraisal aren't about that, so don't make them about that by measuring success that way.

Solutions for Revamping the Performance Management System

Now that we've covered the most common practices that sabotage attempts to revamp the system, let's look at what you should do. Most of these ideas work across the enterprise and for any unit manager who wants to revitalize the way he or she manages performance in a single unit, division, or department.

Applying the Cascade Process

Is there a secret to reaping the benefits of a new, revamped performance management system? Yes, and it's not such a secret. The same method works with most major functional changes across an enterprise. It's called the *cascade process*.

On the surface it's simple. It involves having the people who possess the necessary authority and credibility institute change, in a stepwise fashion. It starts at the top of the hierarchy, not with the HR department.

First, the CEO uses the new system with his or her reports (usually the executive group), tutoring and modeling how to do it (and why), and making it part of the job responsibility for each of these reports to use the same process with their staff (usually unit managers). In turn, these unit managers do the same for their reports, and on down, making sure that each level is held accountable for getting it done.

It's amazing how compelling it is for managers to know they will be evaluated on how well they manage performance using the new system by people with authority and clout. It sends the unambiguous message that those at the top of the hierarchy are serious.

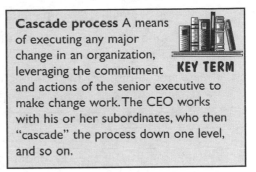

Cascade process A means of executing any major change in an organization, leveraging the commitment **KEY TERM** and actions of the senior executive to make change work. The CEO works with his or her subordinates, who then "cascade" the process down one level, and so on.

This is the only consistently effective way to implement a powerful and beneficial performance management system.

Does it take time for things to pervade the entire organization? Yes. Does it require executive commitment? Yes. Is it worth it? Yes. Do you want results? Then this is the way to make results happen.

Pilots, Testing, Small-Scale Success, and Champions

The cascade process is what you do at implementation time, when you want to move things across the enterprise (or division). That's not the whole story. Other techniques can help before you get to the enterprise-wide rollout.

You need to address inertia and resistance to change early on, prior to rollout, as there is usually some cynicism attached to performance appraisals. For that reason, once you feel you have designed a final system, *pilot* it on a small scale—let's say at a work unit level or small division of the company. Choose the pilot work unit because it's most likely to succeed at the task. That means a strong, credible manager or executive, with good communication skills, someone who is well regarded by his or her employees and who supports the ideas and principles of the new system. Don't pick the most controlling old-school manager; choose a manager with a strong commitment to cooperation and problem solving, who doesn't look for people to blame when something goes wrong.

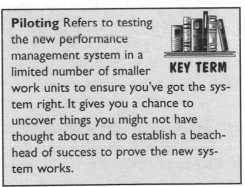

Piloting Refers to testing the new performance management system in a limited number of smaller **KEY TERM** work units to ensure you've got the system right. It gives you a chance to uncover things you might not have thought about and to establish a beachhead of success to prove the new system works.

By piloting or small-scale implementation, you will:

■ Create a model for implementation that works and can be used as a model at enterprise rollout time.

■ Create a champion for the process. When you have a manager who has succeeded with the new system and reaped the benefits, that manager is the best proof of value and can become a helper and support person when the time comes for the rollout. You move the new system from pie-in-the-sky directives from the executive suite to something that is proven in *your* workplace.

Piloting is also an opportunity to test all the parts of the system, from the principles and purposes right down to the … well, pink or green forms. At least it allows testing and revision, and the time to do that is before enterprise rollout.

Input from the Customers of the Performance Management System

Who are the customers of the performance management system? They are the managers and employees who will use the system. OK, they aren't customers in the traditional sense, but in every other way, they are the ones who determine whether the time and effort spent revamping the performance management system is going to be a waste or a success. If you need a definition of "customer" that fits, try this: your customers are the people who will determine the success or failure of anything they are asked to use, whether they pay for something or not. Your customers are also the ones who can cause misery or rejoicing.

Once accepted as the customers of organizational change, their input is required early on, both in the design phase of a new system and for implementation.

As with other endeavors, if the customers (users) of something feel some sense of ownership of the product or service and feel it has real value to them, they are more likely to buy in. By inviting input from them, you increase that buy-in and collect data that makes the system more valuable to the end users. The net gain is that you have users committed to the system because they have been an integral part of its creation and implementation from the start.

Manager's Checklist for Chapter 15

☑ Managers shouldn't make the mistake of waiting for the company to move if they are interested in managing performance more effectively. Individual managers can impact their own units far more easily than a CEO can change the entire enterprise.

☑ Pilot and test your performance management system prior to deployment across the enterprise to make sure you got it right and to create walking, talking success stories.

☑ Be alert to surface changes that obscure the fact that nothing important is changing and remember that organizational inertia will always "fight back." Every time you change the color of the form, but nothing important, you lose credibility in the eyes of employees and other managers.

☑ Cascade everything if the desire is to deploy a new system across the enterprise. Executives commit, execute the system with their reports, who then commit, and execute the system with their reports.

Performance Management in Action

Now that we've covered the principles and process of performance management, what does it look like in action? Remember the story that opened Chapter 1, about Michael and the
Acme Progressive Company? Michael wasn't managing performance
with the 14 staff members who reported to him. Whatever he did probably hurt more than helped. Well, something happened to Michael while
you were reading this book.

He got a new boss. Marie was hired from outside Acme to get the
company on track. Tough, supportive, and talented, she decided things
were too chaotic and it was time to take action.

The First Step Toward Improving Performance Management

Marie asked Michael to schedule a meeting with her to discuss the performance of his department. After some preliminary chitchat, Marie got
to the point: "Michael, I've been looking at the performance of all the
departments in my division and I'm concerned. We're going backward
and we need to turn it around, or Acme is going to be in big trouble. I
need to know from you what you think the problem is with your group."

After some thought, Michael replied: "I know productivity seems to be down, but it's like we have more work and less time. My employees are worn down, and they make a lot of mistakes. Frankly, we could do with more staff."

Marie shook her head and explained that, because of Acme's financial situation, staffing levels had been frozen. She continued: "I know you're busy, but 'busy' isn't the point, is it? Everyone may be working hard, but is it possible that they may not be focusing on the important things they need to do to raise productivity?"

"It's interesting you bring that up," Michael replied. "It looks to me like people are forgetting what's important and not so important. We seem to be spinning our wheels."

TRICKS OF THE TRADE

DIAGNOSIS AND COOPERATION

Notice that Marie isn't telling Michael what to do. She's working with him, asking questions to try to uncover the underlying problem. That's part of diagnosis, whether it's during performance planning or performance appraisal. The goal is to identify barriers to achievement and overcome them together.

"Good," Marie said. "That's my impression also. How are you working with staff to keep them focused on the important work and making sure it gets done efficiently? How are you managing their performance?"

Michael paused, looking a bit embarrassed, and answered: "Well, you know, I'm pretty busy. But we have meetings every two months to talk about the work, and we do that once-a-year thing that the personnel department forces us to do—you know, with those forms to fill out?"

"I know about those forms," Marie sighed. "They make me turn them in, too."

She continued: "That's not enough. We need to do something to help you and your employees, or there are going to be some serious shake-ups.

"Here's what we're going to do. I'd like you to start managing performance with your staff—and it's got to be meaningful. But it's not something you have to do on your own. I'll be doing the same things with all my managers. So, while I'm helping you with your performance, you'll be using the same techniques to help your staff.

"Here's how we're going to start. The vice presidents and I have set a number of goals and objectives for the company for the next year. Each department is expected to contribute to achieving those goals. In about a year you and I are going to sit down and assess whether your department has met that obligation. As the manager, you are accountable and responsible for making sure it happens."

Michael, looking a bit green, said: "Well, OK, I guess that's why I get paid the big bucks. How are you going to measure this? Not with that horrible ratings form, I hope?"

"No," Marie answered. "You and I are going to talk and set objectives for you personally. That's what we'll measure. Those objectives need to be simple and measurable. And we'll develop them together, but mostly you will suggest them, since you know your job best."

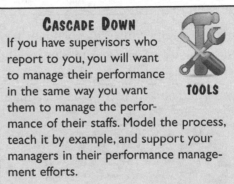

CASCADE DOWN

If you have supervisors who report to you, you will want to manage their performance in the same way you want them to manage the performance of their staffs. Model the process, teach it by example, and support your managers in their performance management efforts.

TOOLS

"And you want me to do the same thing for my staff?"

"Exactly." Marie nodded energetically. "That's how we'll coordinate the company's goals with your department's goals and the objectives for your staff. We'll still have to complete those ratings forms, but I've talked to personnel and they've agreed, for now, to let you add some notes to them. Maybe next year we can convince them to drop the ratings entirely."

Michael felt ready to deal with specifics, so Marie closed the meeting by scheduling another.

"What I'd like you to do," she said, "is take the goals and objectives for the whole company and discuss them with your staff. You and I will get together in three weeks to set your department's goals and your personal objectives and standards, which we'll use to assess your progress at the end of the year. Then, you're going to do something similar with your staff, and you'll measure and manage their performance the same way." She paused. "What do you think?"

"I'm not sure I have much choice," Michael admitted, "but I'll give it a try."

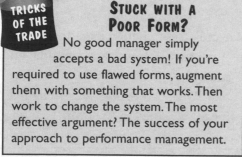

STUCK WITH A POOR FORM?
No good manager simply accepts a bad system! If you're required to use flawed forms, augment them with something that works. Then work to change the system. The most effective argument? The success of your approach to performance management.

After more discussion, Marie gave Michael some material on performance management and writing objectives and standards. Then they scheduled their next meeting.

Michael reviewed the overall goals for the company, and then called a staff meeting. At the meeting, he explained that employees needed to link their individual performance to achieve the goals set for the organization. They all discussed what they would need to do and came up with a set of goals and objectives for the department.

SMART MANAGING

INVOLVE STAFF IN THE BIG PICTURE
It's important that staff understand how they fit in with the success of their department and with the whole organization. By involving staff in determining the best way to contribute to the overall goals, you can make their jobs mean more to them.

Michael closed the meeting by explaining what was to happen next: "I'm taking our goals to Marie to make sure she feels we're aiming at the right bull's-eye. They might change a bit, but I think we have them pretty well nailed down. After speaking with Marie, I'll schedule a meeting with each of you to discuss how your work in the next year ties into our overall goals. At that time, we'll decide how to keep track of progress and determine how we're going to evaluate your work against those objectives."

Agreeing on Goals and Objectives

Three weeks later, Marie and Michael met again. They reviewed the goals and objectives set for the department and finalized them so they aligned with those of the company.

Marie summarized the results. "OK, these are the things we've agreed that you and your department are going to achieve. You need to increase your sales by 10 percent, which seems a realistic goal. We need to limit errors in the ordering system, with our starting goal being one error a month. Also, we want to cut by 50 percent justified customer complaints going to the customer service department."

She paused and looked at Michael. He nodded in agreement. Marie continued.

"One more thing we've agreed on is we can only achieve these goals if you carry out your managerial responsibilities regarding performance management with your staff. Since these are the criteria we're going to use to evaluate your performance, we need to be sure about them. Are these goals clear to you? Do they make sense? Will they get us where we need to go?"

Michael exressed concern. "What happens to me if we do our appraisal and I fall short? I don't know if I can control all these things."

"Good question," Marie replied. "Here's how we'll work it. Once a month you and I will meet for about 15 minutes to discuss progress toward these goals and objectives. If we aren't making progress, we'll figure out how to overcome any obstacles. If necessary we'll include your staff. OK?"

Michael nodded.

"My job is to help you do your job," Marie said, "and your job is to help your staff do theirs. Frankly, I'm not concerned that you won't meet the objectives, because together we can and will do it. To answer your question, I won't be concerned if we miss those targets by a bit, provided we continue to improve. If we don't improve at all, then we'll have to take action, depending on why we haven't. You and I will look at our successes and any failures at your year-end performance review meeting. Then we'll figure out where to go from there."

At the end of the meeting, Marie and Michael listed the objectives and standards that would be used to evaluate Michael and his department. To record their agreement, they had the objectives and standards typed up and had two copies made. Each signed both copies and kept one.

Planning Performance with Staff

Michael met with each employee as Marie had met with him, to establish what each employee should do to contribute to the department's success

SMART MANAGING

SIMPLE DOCUMENTATION

To ensure manager and employee are in agreement, and for legal reasons, it's important to document objectives and standards. Do this simply, listing only the most important things to focus on. It's as important to document what happens in performance planning as it is to document what happens at the performance appraisal.

and to agree on the standards for reviewing their performance. Rather than establish standards himself, Michael asked each person to set their own.

For example, this is how he handled the matter with Sarah, the receptionist and switchboard operator:

"Since we're concerned about customer service, we should decide on what would be the maximum number of rings for any phone call. What would you recommend?"

"Well," Sarah replied, "I don't know."

"Would 50 rings be reasonable?"

"No," she laughed. "That would be much too long."

"Well," Michael asked, "how about two rings?"

"No, that's impossible—not practical."

TRICKS OF THE TRADE

GO TO EXTREMES

If an employee has trouble setting a performance standard, suggest something impractical. Start with an extreme criterion. Then try one at the opposite extreme. Little by little, work through more moderate standards until you can agree on one.

Michael and Sarah continued until eventually they agreed on a target of five rings. They decided to allow some leeway, agreeing that 95 percent of phone calls would be answered within 5 rings and that no call should ever ring more than 15 times, under any

circumstances. They thought this reasonable maximum would greatly reduce complaints about poor phone service.

Before they moved on to the next objective and standard, Michael asked: "Here's the key question. What do you need to be able to meet that standard? What can I do to help?" Sarah suggested a few changes regarding phone coverage during coffee breaks and lunch and recommended buying a low-cost cordless headset so she could answer the phone when she was away from her desk.

At the end of the meeting, Michael and Sarah followed the simple documentation process, recording the tasks, objectives, and standards they'd agreed on.

Michael completed his meetings with each employee, clarifying jobs and standards, and identifying small, inexpensive changes they could make to help meet their objectives. In the process, he discovered a few things.

First, he realized there were a lot of little obstacles and annoyances interfering with productivity—barriers they could remove or minimize with no cash outlay. Second, he found that once staff understood that he was there to help them do their jobs, they were cooperative, even happy with the process. Several times, at the end of meetings, employees asked why Acme had waited so long before starting performance management.

Communicating About Progress and Solving Problems

During the year, Michael met regularly with employees to review their progress. Each month, in 10-minute, one-on-one meetings, he and each employee addressed two questions:

1. How are you progressing in meeting your goals?
2. What problems are you encountering?

In some cases, Michael noted the difficulties encountered. Sometimes a staff member needed to upgrade his or her skills, so Michael provided training and coaching. As time went on, he found it necessary to change some of the objectives and standards, because the company altered its priorities. Sometimes responsibilities shifted; some were added, and some eliminated. After each series of meetings with his staff, Michael met with Marie to update her and discuss his responsibilities with her as each of his employees had done with him.

> **DYNAMIC GOALS AND STANDARDS**
> **TRICKS OF THE TRADE**
> Never etch your goals and standards in stone. Be flexible enough on an individual basis so the department can react to company shifts. Progress meetings are a good place to determine changes were needed.

Preparing for the Yearly Review

March 31 marked the end of Acme Progressive's fiscal year. One of Michael's responsibilities was to do a year-end performance review with each of his staff members. Since Michael knew he was going to be evaluated on those reviews, he was well motivated. Here's how he handled the reviews.

At a general staff meeting in late February, Michael reminded his employees that it was time to schedule meetings to discuss the past year's performance and plan their performance for the next year.

"As you know, we've been working to improve our overall performance and meeting regularly to do that. It looks to me as if we've succeeded in clearing out some barriers and meeting our departmental goals. What we need to do next is discuss problems you faced in meeting your individual objectives and decide where we need to go for the next year.

"Since I've been meeting regularly with you, I don't expect any surprises. You all know where you stand, so we only need to do some paperwork and plan. I'd like you to look at the performance planning notes we made in our individual meetings and other notes, you might have from our regular progress meetings.

"When I meet with you, I'm going to ask whether you feel you've hit the targets we set together and, just as we have done in our progress meetings, we'll look to remove barriers. We'll make some notes, and each of us will sign them. Of course, we'll also complete that rating form required for personnel. But we'll focus on the goals we negotiated."

Reviewing and Evaluating

In March, Michael met with each employee. He tried to speak very little, be as helpful as possible, and encourage the employee to evaluate his or her progress. For the most part, it worked well. There were no surprises for anyone.

In one instance, however, there was a problem. Fred had consistently missed the targets he'd set with Michael. Because Fred and Michael had been meeting regularly, both anticipated a problem. How did Michael handle this?

First, he and Fred established that there was a performance gap. Michael used notes from the progress meetings to inform the discussion. He started a diagnostic process to determine what had been causing the problem, as they'd done in their monthly meetings. They agreed that Michael would continue to coach Fred.

Although Michael was generally supportive, he had to make sure Fred understood that both he and the company were serious about meeting performance goals.

Here's what he said:

"Fred, I'll continue to work with you. You've met some of your objectives and sometimes even surpassed what we asked of you. That tells me you have the ability to meet the rest of them in the new year. Please come to me if you have difficulties, and we'll continue to meet regularly. It might be, though, that you would be more successful in a job that builds on your strengths; that's something you and I need to look at if you miss your targets in the next quarter.

"So we don't lose sight of the issues, I've outlined our course of action. We'll both sign this paper, but I'm going to hold onto it for another three months. If you hit your interim targets for the next quarter and the next year, I'll destroy the notes. If you miss your targets, the notes and documentation will go into your personnel file, and we'll need to figure out what to do next."

Fred reluctantly agreed.

The Outcomes

How does the story end? In fact, it never ends. The performance management process begins anew. The appraisals not only end the year but also begin the planning process for the next year. Let's summarize the outcomes.

Michael and his boss, Marie, met to do his appraisal. The results were good, although not news. Michael's department and Michael had met or surpassed all the goals. Marie and Michael were so pleased with the positive results that they met with the vice president of human resources to discuss their success and ask that everyone at Acme be given more flexibility. Personnel finally got rid of the required ratings forms.

The policy of "no surprises" worked well. Michael and his staff identified barriers early on and overcame most of them. Employees knew where they stood during the year, and Michael had the information he needed. On a corporate level, everyone benefited by linking individual and departmental objectives to the overall company goals.

What about Fred? In a perfect world, Fred would have met his next year's objectives. Unfortunately, Fred continued to struggle despite everyone's efforts to help. Eventually Michael met with Fred and the personnel department to see if another job at Acme would be more suitable. That way the company could salvage its investment in Fred (the cost of hiring, training, etc.). Fred chose to move (with great relief) to another position where he could succeed. Could Acme have let Fred go? Yes, the firm had sufficient documentation to support that option—as a last resort.

Closing Comments

Performance management is in some ways simple and in other ways complex. It consists of lots of parts, and it requires some skills. But if you approach it with the proper mindset, you can make it work—and it will pay great benefits.

Manager's Checklist for Chapter 16

☑ Performance management is about people, communication, dialogue, and working together, not about forms or forcing employees to produce.

☑ Performance management is an ongoing process throughout the year. It's not solely about performance appraisal. In fact, performance appraisal is only a small part.

☑ Performance management is about preventing and solving problems, not about punishing or blaming. By identifying problems and their cause, you can work with staff to solve them.

☑ Aim for "no surprises." There shouldn't be any surprises for staff during appraisals, and there should be no surprises for you regarding their progress.

Epilogue

This may be my last "normal book" on performance management, but I'm not done yet. While I've tried to make this as complete as possible, there are other topics that couldn't fit into this book. For example, what about 360-degree feedback? Or how to use the many sophisticated software packages so they help rather than hinder?

I want to invite readers to use our free Internet resource center on all things related to performance management and improving productivity. The address: http://performance-appraisals.org.

We've indexed over 1,000 relevant articles available free on the Internet, created a specialized search engine to help you find other management resources, and of course, there are my own writings. We pride ourselves on being the largest repository of information on performance management and appraisal on the planet. The intent is simple: get into your hands the best material with no hassle, no registration, and no fees.

Now, here's a secret. I'm planning a book that will both entertain and enlighten readers on this topic. I don't know about you, but reading about performance management sometimes (this book excepted) can make my eyes roll around in my head. It's not an exciting topic, and now that you've finished the book, I tender my congratulations at reading most of the words. I trust it was useful.

Be that as it may, the new project involves some nifty storytelling, humor, and even some history to entertain you as you continue to learn about management and organizations. I plan a whole series of these "teaching epics," all with some familiar yet amusing characters. You know—how to improve customer service, strategic planning, and of course, performance management—practical stuff that's fun to read and easy to use.

This is yet another reason to stay tuned to our Performance Management Resource Center. Sorry I can't share more, but ... publishers may belly up to the bar for first shot at this mystery series.

Index